D-DAY

THE AIR AND SEA INVASION OF NORMANDY IN PHOTOS

NICHOLAS A. VERONICO

STACKPOLE
BOOKS

Guilford, Connecticut

Published by Stackpole Books
An imprint of The Rowman & Littlefield Publishing Group, Inc.
4501 Forbes Blvd., Ste. 200
Lanham, MD 20706
www.rowman.com

Distributed by NATIONAL BOOK NETWORK
(800) 462-6420

Copyright © 2019 by Nicholas A. Veronico

British Library Cataloguing in Publication Information available

Library of Congress Cataloging-in-Publication Data available

ISBN 978-0-8117-3809-5 (hardcover)
ISBN 978-0-8117-6813-9 (e-book)

♾™ The paper used in this publication meets the minimum requirements of American National Standard for Information Sciences—Permanence of Paper for Printed Library Materials, ANSI/NISO Z39.48-1992.

Printed in the United States of America

CONTENTS

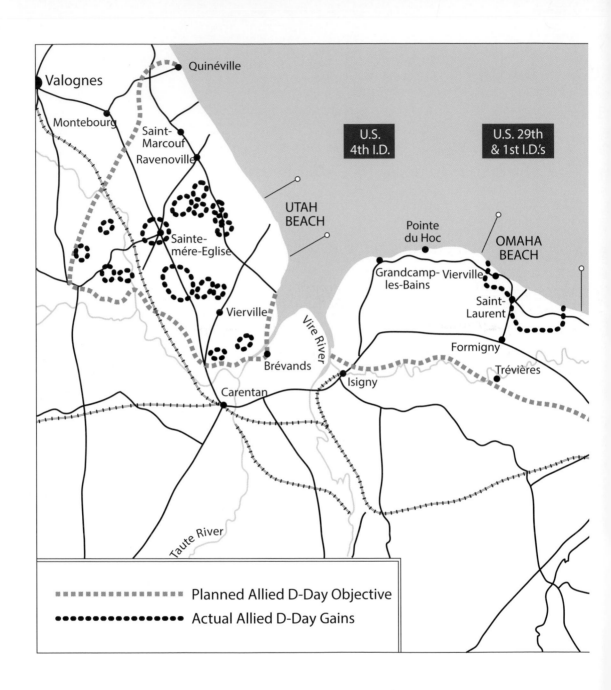

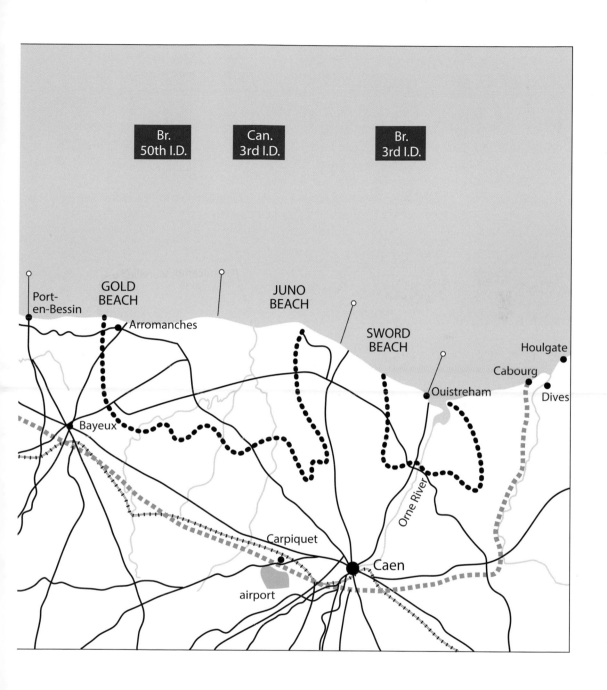

Operation Overlord: The D-Day Invasion of France

The war in Europe had raged since the German invasion of Poland on September 1, 1939, and the United States joined the struggle against the Axis powers on December 7, 1941, when the Japanese attacked the American fleet at Pearl Harbor. During the years leading up to the Allies' cross-Channel invasion of the European continent, millions of lives had been lost, and the Allies would accept nothing less than unconditional surrender from Germany and Japan. The third Axis nation, Italy, was invaded on July 9, 1943, and subsequently surrendered on September 8, 1943.

After months of preparation, planning, and stockpiling of men, ships, and weapons, the Allies were ready to assault the European continent. From January to May 1944, more than 589,000 men arrived in the United Kingdom in advance of the invasion. The Germans expected the Allies to come ashore at Calais on the French coast, as this is the narrowest point along the Strait of Dover between England and France, and had heavily reinforced the Atlantic seawall with a vast network of shore batteries, beach obstacles, and minefields.

The Allies instead chose to invade the European continent along the Normandy region coastline in the Bay of the Seine, roughly between Le Havre in the north and Cherbourg on the Cotentin Peninsula in the south. After months of training soldiers in how to assault the beaches and sailors in how to handle landing craft and larger amphibious ships, a target date was set for Operation Neptune—the amphibious assault phase of Operation Overlord (the invasion of France).

Gen. Dwight D. Eisenhower was selected as Supreme Commander of the Allied Expeditionary Force. Managing the naval aspect of the invasion was Adm. Sir Bertram Ramsay (Royal Navy), who served as Supreme Naval Commander for the operation. Two men were responsible for getting the troops to the beaches: Rear Adm. Alan G. Kirk commanded the Western Naval Task Force, landing American troops on the beaches code-named "Utah" and "Omaha"; Rear Adm. Sir Philip Vian (Royal Navy) commanded the Eastern Naval Task Force that landed Commonwealth troops at "Gold," "Juno," and "Sword" Beaches.

BEACH INTEL

Tides in the Bay of the Seine where the invasion would take place were very complex. When the tide rises from low to high water, the change in depth can be as much as 5 feet per hour, and the difference in area between high and low tide can cover more than 20 feet.

Allied naval forces had to know the tidal movements and ranges for each invasion beach. To obtain this data, predictions were made by the Intelligence Division, Office of the Chief Engineer, European Theater of Operations, US Army. The predictions were collated into estimated tide tables, which were then given to photo reconnaissance pilots who overflew the beaches recording the position of the tides and the times of the movements. The reconnaissance photos were then compared with the tidal estimates to provide an accurate picture of when the waterline would reach specific points on each of the assault beaches. The tidal timing developed by the Office of the Chief Engineer set the timescale for Operation Overlord. The majority of the images used to make the Overlord tidal maps were captured by the photo reconnaissance Spitfires (PR Mk XI) of No. 16 Squadron and the Mosquitos (PR Mk IX and XVI) of No. 140 Squadron, 34th Wing, Royal Air Force.

The tide tables also gave planners a good estimate as to when the German anti-invasion obstacles would be covered by the sea and to what depth, or when they would be exposed and easy for the landing craft to avoid. However, landing on the beach at low tide would expose the invading troops to greater fire from the defenders. Whatever path was chosen, men would be put into harm's way.

INVADING THE CONTINENT

The invasion troops were boarded on ships at every dock, beach, and pier in southern England on May 28. US forces were supported by and transported in 931 ships, while the British and Commonwealth Armies sailed in 1,796 ships of all types. The invasion ships were ready on June 3, but the weather was not cooperating. June 4 was no better, and June 5 was predicted to be miserable too. Forecasters predicted a break in the weather on June 6, and close to midnight on June 4 General Eisenhower gave the invasion order: D-Day was set for the morning of June 6. The invasion armada sortied from the coast of England on the morning of June 5.

During the early-morning hours of June 6, more than 13,000 American and 8,500 British paratroopers landed behind the beaches. They were to capture vital bridges and secure beach exits to enable soldiers of the seaborne assault to move inland as quickly as possible. Offshore, at 2:00 a.m., minesweepers moved in, clearing channels for the fire support and amphibious ships that were soon to follow.

At 6:00 a.m., as ships of the invasion fleet approached the landing areas, German heavy coastal batteries opened up, firing at the approaching invasion fleet.

Facing the soldiers coming ashore were beach obstacles designed to snare landing craft, anti-ship mines, antipersonnel mines along the beaches and down to the tide line, one armored division, two mobile infantry divisions, and three additional divisions of vehicle-less infantry. Six armored divisions plus the German Fifteenth Army were within a day's march of reinforcing the army at the beachhead.

Allied troops began reaching the beach at 6:30 a.m. to face withering fire from the German defenders. *LCI-93, LCI-553,* and *LCT-612* were shelled by shore batteries and subsequently sank. The quiet weapon—undersea mines—took a heavy toll: Destroyer *Corry* (DD-463), anti-submarine patrol craft PC-1261, eleven tank landing craft, and five infantry landing craft were quickly sent to the bottom. Casualties from these ships were enormous, and those who survived had a long swim to the beach, if they could shed their full combat gear, or hoped for rescue by surrounding vessels. In spite of German resistance, both active and passive, more than 21,000 men and more than 1,700 tanks, half-tracks, trucks, and jeeps were ashore at Utah Beach by 6:00 p.m.

German casemated gun emplacements were the target of the day for Allied fire-support ships. Gun fire support was called for by Army units on the ground, and the fall of the shot was monitored by Navy pilots flying from land bases in Britain.

American troops faced stiffer resistance and increased German fortifications at Omaha Beach. Troops here endured a long trip over open sand, liberally sown with antipersonnel mines, to a concrete seawall topped with barbed wire.

To afford the soldiers tactical surprise, the Normandy beaches did not receive any pre-invasion bombardment, either by air or by ship, in the weeks prior to the assault. All the German defenses were intact. On the morning of D-Day, shore bombardment by the destroyers, cruisers, and battleships of the invasion fleet turned the tide of battle at Omaha Beach. Firing on targets, often within yards of American troops, many of the destroyers closed to within 800 yards of the beach—frequently touching bottom. As the troops moved away from the beaches, gunfire support ships were hitting targets as far as 10 miles inland.

The Allied armies ashore consolidated their position and soon began moving across the French countryside. The Luftwaffe moved aircraft from Italy and Germany to counter the invasion fleet. They used radio-guided bombs, employed with success off the coast of Italy, but Allied air superiority over the French coast limited their effectiveness. German undersea mines continued to extract a high toll for sailing in French coastal waters, sinking or heavily damaging a number of ships before the area was cleared.

To supply the advancing armies, the British devised two types of emergency harbors to be constructed off the invasion beaches. "Mulberry A" was constructed at Omaha Beach using concrete caissons that had been floated across the Channel from England and flooded, sinking into position to form a breakwater. "Mulberry B" was built off Gold Beach near Arromanches. "Gooseberry" harbors were built at both Omaha and Utah Beaches by sinking obsolete or war-weary ships in 40 feet of water to form a breakwater. Small craft were able to operate or take shelter from the sea behind the gooseberries. The artificial harbors proved their worth on the night of June 18–19, when strong winds and heavy seas wreaked havoc on the hundreds of ships and small craft supporting the invasion. The storm lasted for three days and completely wrecked Mulberry A.

GENERAL EISENHOWER'S MESSAGE TO THE EUROPEAN PEOPLE

People of Western Europe:

A landing was made this morning on the coast of France by troops of the Allied Expeditionary Force. This landing is part of the concerted United Nations' plan for the liberation of Europe, made in conjunction with our great Russian allies.

I have this message for all of you. Although the initial assault may not have been made in your own country, the hour of your liberation is approaching.

All patriots, men and women, young and old, have a part to play in the achievement of final victory. To members of resistance movements, I say, "Follow the instructions you have received." To patriots who are not members of organized resistance groups, I say, "Continue your passive resistance, but do not needlessly endanger your lives until I give you the signal to rise and strike the enemy. The day will come when I shall need your united strength." Until that day, I call on you for the hard task of discipline and restraint.

Citizens of France! I am proud to have again under my command the gallant Forces of France. Fighting beside their Allies, they will play a worthy part in the liberation of their Homeland.

Because the initial landing has been made on the soil of your country, I repeat to you with even greater emphasis my message to the peoples of other occupied countries in Western Europe. Follow the instructions of your leaders. A premature uprising of all Frenchmen may prevent you from being of maximum help to your country in the critical hour. Be patient. Prepare!

As Supreme Commander of the Allied Expeditionary Force, there is imposed on me the duty and responsibility of taking all measures necessary to the prosecution of the war. Prompt and willing obedience to the orders that I shall issue is essential.

Effective civil administration of France must be provided by Frenchmen. All persons must continue in their present duties unless otherwise instructed. Those who have made common cause with the enemy and so betrayed their country will be removed. As France is liberated from her oppressors, you yourselves will choose your representatives, and the government under which you wish to live.

In the course of this campaign for the final defeat of the enemy, you may sustain further loss and damage. Tragic though they may be, they are part of the price of victory. I assure you that I shall do all in my power to mitigate your hardships. I know that I can count on your steadfastness now, no less than in the past. The heroic deeds of Frenchmen who have continued the struggle against the Nazis and their Vichy satellites, in France and throughout the French Empire, have been an example and an inspiration to all of us.

This landing is but the opening phase of the campaign in Western Europe. Great battles lie ahead. I call upon all who love freedom to stand with us. Keep your faith staunch—our arms are resolute—together we shall achieve victory.

—Gen. Dwight D. Eisenhower
Supreme Commander
Allied Expeditionary Force
Radio broadcast, 10:00 a.m., June 6, 1944

Operation Neptune was concluded on June 25 when US Navy battleships disabled the Fermanville battery (known to the Germans as the Hamburg battery), part of the coastal defense network surrounding the city of Cherbourg. The Fermanville battery's four 280mm cannon, with a range of 40,000 yards, harassed Allied shipping until battleships *Texas* and *Arkansas* began to slug it out with the German battery. One cannon was put out of action before the Navy declared the duel a draw. Cherbourg fell on June 26 and, after small pockets of resistance were mopped up, the Cotentin Peninsula came completely under Allied control. The Fermanville battery fell on June 28.

From Normandy, the land battle began working its way across France, with the Germans fighting to hold every yard of ground. Eleven hard-fought months later, the Allies accepted the unconditional surrender of the Germans on May 7, 1945.

Gen. Dwight D. Eisenhower, Supreme Allied Commander of the Allied Expeditionary Force, addresses members of the 101st Airborne Division on June 5, 1944. Eisenhower had overseen the invasion of North Africa and the invasion of Sicily, and in January 1944 was designated Supreme Allied Commander of the Allied Expeditionary Force. In this new role, Eisenhower had to fight an interservice political battle with members of the US military as well as with Allied commanders and politicians. He eventually gained the control necessary to build a cohesive fighting force that could defeat the Nazis.

Closest to the general is 1st Lt. Wallace C. Strobel, along with members of the 502nd Parachute Infantry Regiment. The 502nd secured two causeways across the marshes behind Utah Beach and destroyed a 122mm German coastal defense battery at Saint-Martin-de-Varreville. LIBRARY OF CONGRESS

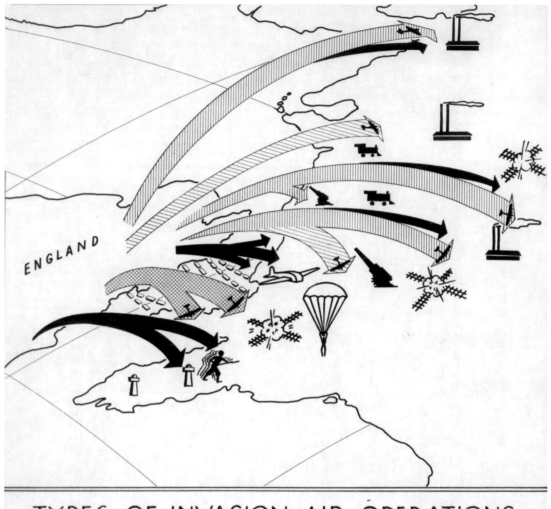

TYPES OF INVASION AIR OPERATIONS

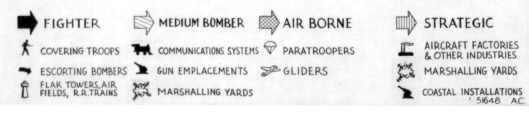

Above and facing page: Graphic representations of how the Allies would execute an invasion of the European continent. Strategic and tactical targets are outlined, and paratroop and glider-borne forces are represented. The higher-fidelity view provides target detail and acknowledges the cooperation of underground forces. NARA/USAAF 51648AC AND 51649AC

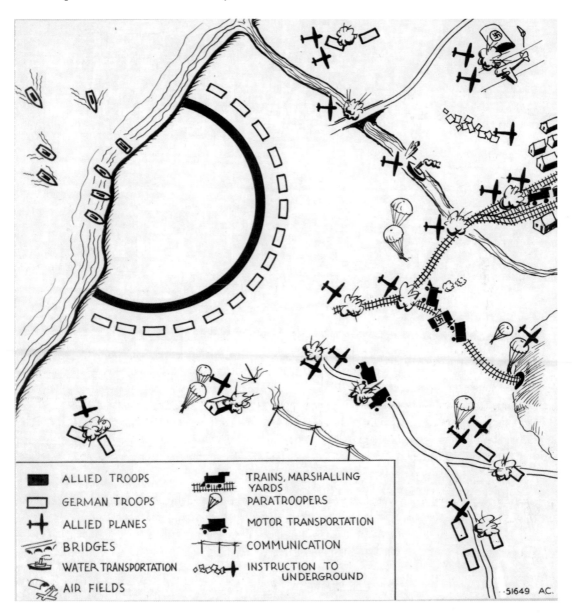

The Atlantic Wall in France was the location for much of Nazi Germany's super artillery.
Along the Calais section of coast, only 32 miles across the Channel from Dover, England,
the Germans had sited nineteen cannon of 190mm or larger, including three 406mm guns at
Battery Lindemann that had a range of 35 miles. General Field Marshal Gerd von Rundstedt
had begun the work to improve defenses along the Atlantic Wall, but it was not until January
1944 that Erwin Rommel, seen here at left, could begin to make serious improvements. He had
six months to lay mines, dig tank traps, fill the fields with "Rommel's Asparagus" to deter gliders
from landing in open fields, and fill the beaches with anti-invasion obstacles. BUNDESARCHIV

Left: Shortly before the invasion, German meteorologists predicted
that the weather would be poor for the next two weeks and that an
invasion was unlikely. Having that information, Field Marshal Rommel
and other high-ranking military commanders in the area went on leave
or on training exercises. After the invasion, he returned to Normandy,
where he conferred with his superior, General Field Marshal Gerd
von Rundstedt, and his chief of staff, Gen. Hans Speidel. All three
were convinced that Normandy was a diversion and, based on faulty
information coming from Allied deception measures, believed that the
main invasion would come at Calais.

On July 17, 1944, Rommel was returning to his headquarters at
La Roche-Guyon, 40 miles (65 km) outside Paris, when his staff car
was strafed by a Spitfire from the Royal Canadian Air Force's No.
412 Squadron piloted by Flight Lt. Charles W. "Charley" Fox. Rommel
was seriously injured in the attack.

Field Marshal Rommel was implicated in the July 20, 1944, bomb
plot to kill Adolf Hitler, and was subsequently given the choice, on
October 14, 1944, to commit suicide or face a public trial. Rommel
chose to swallow cyanide. His death was followed by a state funeral.

BUNDESARCHIV BILD 101-719-0223-20

SLAPTON SANDS REHEARSAL

In preparation for the Normandy invasion, soldiers had to be familiar with the workings of the landing craft and how to rush the beach. Rehearsal landings at Slapton Sands, east of Plymouth, in April and May 1944, were code-named "Operation Tiger." These rehearsals gave soldiers and sailors the opportunity to work together, learn how to embark and disembark from landing craft and troop ships, and learn how to communicate across different styles and equipment. Here a group of four M4 Sherman tanks with extended air intakes come ashore near *LCT(5)-413* on the Slapton Sands beach. *LCT-413* was assigned to Assault Group O-4 and was slated to deliver US Army Rangers and DUKW trucks to the Pointe du Hoc area on June 6. NHHC 80-G-251992

Below: LCTs race toward the beach as amphibious M4 Sherman tanks wade ashore at Slapton Sands. The Sherman tanks were deployed during an earlier round and are practicing the transition from the water up the beach. NHHC 80-G-251999

Facing page top: This panoramic view of the Slapton Sands area shows the size of the invasion rehearsal effort. The Slapton Sands barrier beach, where the troops and vehicles are coming ashore, encloses Slapton Ley, a freshwater lagoon. Aside from its remote location, the undersea topography of the Slapton Sands area was similar to that of Normandy, making it ideal for invasion rehearsals. The name Slapton Sands is a misnomer, as the beach is predominantly flint and quartz shingle. NHHC 80-G-252149

Facing page bottom: *LCT-149* and *LCT-495* on the beach at Slapton Sands with LCIs paralleling the beach behind. *LCT-495* has just unloaded a number of trucks. Notice the coiled strips of branches used to give vehicles traction on the area's soft sand and mud. NHHC 80-G-K-1183

Above: Powered by three 2,000-horsepower, twenty-cylinder Mercedes MB 501 diesel engines, the German *Schnellboot* (S-boat) was 114 feet, 10 inches (35 m) in length, with a beam of 16 feet, 9 inches (5 m) and a top speed of 43 knots. This type of torpedo boat (known to the Allies as an "E-boat," for "enemy boat") attacked the invasion rehearsal fleet off the coast of Slapton Sands. The S-boats that made the attack were from *5.Schnellbootflottille*, which was equipped with S-100 class boats fitted with a pair of bow-mounted torpedo tubes, three 20mm cannon (one in the bow and one on each side amidships), and a 37mm gun on the stern.

During the early-morning hours of April 28, nine S-boats attacked the eight LSTs of Convoy T-4 in Lyme Bay, near Portland, England. Due to a communications error, the convoy was accompanied by only the corvette HMS *Azalea*. A replacement escort was steaming to join the convoy, but that was when the S-boats struck, sinking *LST-507* and *LST-531*. *LST-289* took a torpedo in the stern but was able to limp back to port. The S-boat attack cost the lives of 749 Allied servicemen. BUNDESARCHIV BILD 248-224

Facing page: *LST-289* limps into Dartmouth Harbour midday on April 28 after having been attacked by German torpedo boats in Lyme Bay. Shortly after the attack began, *LST-289* dodged a pair of torpedoes and was nearly struck by damaged *LST-507*. Commanding officer Lt. Harry A. Mettler (USNR) began zigzagging the ship at four- to five-minute intervals, and at 2:28 a.m., four port 40mm and three port 20mm cannon began firing at a fast white boat, similar to a British ML (motor launch) boat.

A third torpedo struck the LST in the stern toward the starboard side. The entire stern of *LST-289* was demolished by the German torpedo's explosion. The aft starboard 40mm gun tub was blown up and onto davit number five, while the aft deckhouse and gun tubs were pushed up and over the navigation bridge aft of the signal bridge.

Onboard the ship were 395 Army officers and men, 22 DUKWs, a 2.5-ton CCKW truck, and 1 jeep. Four men were killed, eight missing, and eighteen wounded (one of whom subsequently died in the hospital). *LST-289* was transferred to the Royal Navy on November 30, 1944, and was sold to the Netherlands Navy on January 30, 1947. NHHC 80-G-K-2054, 80-G-K-2055, AND 80-G-257909

LST-507 photographed by an airship from Blimp Squadron 11 (*ZP-11*) while crossing the Atlantic Ocean en route to England in preparation for the D-Day assault. The LST is carrying an LCT on its deck. On the morning of April 28, one torpedo struck *LST-507* but failed to explode, and a second impacted the auxiliary engine room. The torpedo knocked out the ship's electrical service, which cut the pumps and prevented the crew from fighting the fires. As the fires grew, they quickly consumed vehicles, gasoline, and ammunition stored below decks.

Lt. John H. Doyle (USN), commanding officer of *LST-515,* disobeyed orders and returned to rescue survivors of the sinking *LST-507.* The majority of *LST-507* sank, with the bow remaining above the surface. Gunfire from a British destroyer finished off the ship, sending her to the bottom. When the survivors were counted, it was determined that 424 men had perished in the sinking of *LST-507.* NHHC 80-G-225794

PRE-INVASION BOMBING AND STRAFING

The 381st Bomb Group, based at Ridgewell, England, struck the Brétigny-sur-Orge Airfield at Avord, France, twice as part of the Allies' pre-invasion air superiority campaign. Douglas Long Beach, California-built B-17G-25, serial number 42-38004, *Old Man Tucker*, is seen on the February 5, 1944, mission to Brétigny-sur-Orge Airfield to destroy the Ju 88As of *Kampfgeschwader* 6 (KG 6). During the D-Day invasion and on subsequent days, KG 6 laid mines and attacked ships off the landing beaches. NARA/USAAF

B-17G-10, serial number 42-31330, *Dog Breath*, drops a load of bombs on Bordeaux, France, on March 27, 1944, as the Allies began softening up the French coast while simultaneously bombing targets to give the Germans the wrong impression of where the invasion of the continent would take place. Less than two weeks after D-Day, on June 19, *Dog Breath* was hit by flak in the number-one engine while bombing the Corme-Écluse Airfield, north of Bordeaux and 20 miles inland from the coast near Royan. While the crew battled the engine fire and runaway propeller on engine number one, the number-two engine seized, was shut down, and the propeller feathered to maintain altitude. Pilot 2nd Lt. Clark G. Graham pointed the bomber south and landed at Luceni, Zaragoza, Spain, where the entire ten-man crew was interned for the duration of the war. NARA/USAAF 61732AC

Facing page top: An Eighth Air Force Consolidated Fort Worth, Texas-built B-24H-20, serial number 42-50318, *Satan's Little Sister*, from the 446th Bomb Group, 706th Bomb Squadron based at Bungay, Suffolk, England, drops bombs on the Luftwaffe airfield at Orléans, France, in support of the D-Day operations. Two months later, on August 26, 1944, after dropping its bombload on target at Ludwigshafen, Germany, *Satan's Little Sister* was struck by antiaircraft fire in both the number- two and -three engines as she crossed the Dutch/Belgian border. The aircraft crashed at Roosendaal, the Netherlands, with six of the crew perishing, three taken prisoner, and two evading capture. NARA/USAAF 81185AC

Facing page bottom: B-17s and B-24s from the Fifteenth Air Force in Italy put pressure on the Germans from the south, and here an unidentified Fifteenth Air Force B-17G is seen crossing the French coast. The Fifteenth Air Force was equipped with four bomb wings of B-24s (47th, 49th, 55th, and 304th), while the 5th Bomb Wing operated six B-17 bomb groups (2nd, 97th, 99th, 301st, 463rd, and 483rd). From bases in the heel of the Italian boot, Fifteenth Air Force bombers could attack strategic targets all across northern Europe. NARA/USAAF 122968AC

As part of the Allied efforts to mislead the Germans about where the invasion would take place, heavy bombers softened up the beach areas around Boulogne, France. Boulogne is only 22 miles (35 km) south of the port city of Calais. The short distance between England's ports and the Calais area of France made it the obvious choice for an invasion landing site. The Germans held to this belief, while the Allies had no intention of sending their armies into the meat grinder that would be the Calais beaches. They continued the deception by bombing the Calais area up until the last minute. Note the bombing pattern on the shoreline at lower left. This B-17F, from the 100th Bomb Group (Square D), 351st Bomb Squadron, based at Thorpe Abbotts, England, is seen on D-Day Minus One. NARA/USAAF 51591AC

The double roadway bridge over the Seine River at Rouen, France, was dropped by US bombers on May 27 and 28, a little more than a week before the invasion of the continent. Rouen was an ancient city, and one of France's most beautiful. It was also a transportation hub with road and rail bridges and, at one time, bustling river port facilities. The Germans took the city in 1940, and as the date for the invasion approached, Rouen's importance as an enemy transportation hub was not lost on the Allies. They began a campaign against transportation targets in the region, as well as military targets around the city. Unfortunately, many bombs fell within residential areas and in the old part of the city. The Rouen Cathedral, seen at right in the background, was heavily damaged. In the coming days, as the Germans erected temporary bridges, Thunderbolts and Mustangs returned to knock them down. The town was finally taken by Canadian troops on August 30. NARA/USAAF K-2785

The remains of a German Wasserman-S early-warning radar station in Normandy. This system was composed of eight stacked Freya antennas fitted onto a 200-foot (60 m) mast. It operated on the 120 to 150 MHz bands and had a range in excess of 150 miles (241 km). The size of the structure to stabilize the antenna as well as the adjacent underground bunker is impressive. This bunker has taken a number of direct shell hits above the entryway. NARA/USAAF 72643AC AND 72644AC

Two views of a German Giant Wurzburg (FuSE 65) radar that has received attention from Allied Thunderbolts and Typhoon fighter-bombers. It is being inspected by US Army personnel on June 22, 1944. This FuSE 65 radar was part of the five-antenna complex at Douvres-la-Délivrande, behind the Juno invasion beaches. The 3rd Canadian Infantry Division fought the German defenders for twelve days before finally taking the installation. NARA/USAAF 72626AC AND A-72626AC

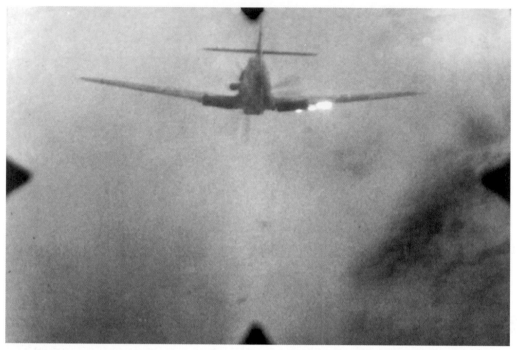

Gun camera still of a Bf 109's final moments as a P-51 pours lead into the starboard wing. A number of factors—lack of fuel and oil, constantly strafed airbases, and Allied air superiority—saw the once-dominant Bf 109s go from hunter to hunted as the war progressed. NARA/USAAF

A Messerschmitt Me 210 twin-engine ground attack fighter comes to grief in a cloud of dust in a French field. The Me 210 was a formidable fighter-bomber fitted with two 20mm cannon and two 7.92mm machine guns facing forward. It could also carry two 1,100-pound (500 kg) bombs. NARA/USAAF B-52398AC

P-47 Thunderbolt pilot Maj. Frank H. Peppers flew seventy-five missions escorting strategic bombers over Germany. Upon completion of his tour, he transferred to the Ninth Air Force's 362nd Fighter Group, 377th Fighter Squadron, flying close air support missions for Gen. George S. Patton's Third Army in the days following the invasion. Peppers was responsible for dropping fifteen single- and double-span railroad bridges, and is seen chalking up another on the side of his P-47's fuselage. Ninth Air Force commanding general Maj. Gen. Hoyt S. Vandenberg dubbed Major Peppers the "Champion Bridge Buster of the Ninth Air Force." NARA/USAAF 57092AC

A pair of Royal Air Force Hawker Typhoons attack a rail line in Normandy. The pair of 60-pound rockets streak for the track as a second and third pair are fired. The first pair hit the tracks dead center. NARA/USAAF 52921AC

This enemy truck dared venture out onto the road during daylight hours and was destroyed by an Eighth Air Force fighter. With the Eighth able to put up more than 1,000 fighters for a sweep, German troops took their lives in their hands when moving on the roads of France. NARA/USAAF 54463AC

SURVEILLANCE ALONG THE ATLANTIC WALL

Once the domain of swimmers and holidaymakers, the beach at Dinard, France, like most cities lining the German's Atlantic Wall, is covered in anti-invasion obstacles. As seen here at low tide, the obstacles were extensive and could easily destroy a landing craft that might encounter them. US ARMY SIGNAL CORPS 192623-S

Above left and right: Utah Beach, photographed from a very low-flying P-38 Lightning, shows "hedgehogs" partially buried by sand brought in with the tides. The hedgehogs appear to be sinking, with many buried up to their crossmembers, while other obstacles are losing the battle against the tide.

INTELLIGENCE DIVISION, OFFICE OF THE CHIEF ENGINEER, ETO, US ARMY

Close-up of the Czech hedgehogs on the beach at Mers-les-Bains, north of Dieppe. These hedgehogs sit at the surf line, blocking access to the wide beach to the right. The beach fronts the town of Mers-les-Bains and shows the extent of Atlantic Wall preparations.

BUNDESARCHIV BILD 101I-297-1719-22

Rommel made extensive use of mines as part of the Atlantic Wall's defenses. Here a beach near Calais is dotted with timber topped with Teller mines. Teller mines were detonated when a boat or vehicle contacted its pressure detonator. BUNDESARCHIV BILD 101I-719-0240-03

Farther up the coast, northwest of Dieppe, photo reconnaissance aircraft flew dangerously close to German positions to obtain intelligence on coastal defenses, troop positions, and potential landing grounds. Here 1st Lt. Albert Lanker from the Ninth Air Force's 10th Photographic Group (Reconnaissance), based at Chalgrove, England, flies his F-5 Lightning low enough to observe gun positions, guns in caves facing the water, and barbed-wire defenses at the top of the cliffs. This photo was taken on May 6, 1944, exactly one month before the D-Day invasion. NARA/USAAF 57354AC

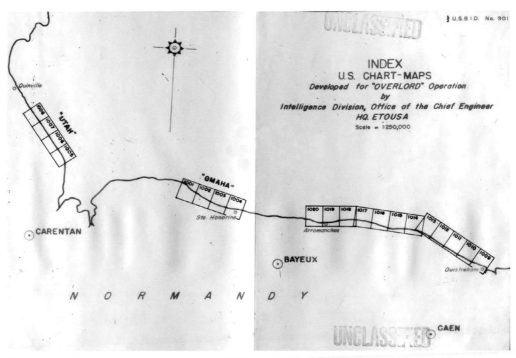

For cartographic purposes, the invasion beaches were divided into blocks for which navigation charts and time tables were developed. The American invasion beaches, Omaha and Utah, are to the left, with Gold (1017 to 1020), Juno (1013 to 1016), and Sword (1009 to 1012) Beaches to the right. Within Gold were beaches code-named "How," "Item," "Jig," and "King"; Juno had "Mike," and "Nan"; Sword's were named "Oboe," "Peter," "Queen," and "Roger." The American's landed on Utah's Tare Green, Uncle Red, and Victor Beaches; while at Omaha men went ashore on Charlie, Dog Green, Dog White, Dog Red, Easy Green, Easy Red, and Fox Green Beaches. INTELLIGENCE DIVISION, OFFICE OF THE CHIEF ENGINEER, ETO, US ARMY

Aerial view of Omaha Beach at low tide on April 22, 1944, showing four distinct sandbars (indicated by numbers 1–4) and a corresponding number of runnels (letters A–D). From this information, the invasion planners had to make decisions considering myriad details and scenarios. For example, if the landing craft came in when the tide was too low, they would ground on the first bar and the soldiers would have to swim through the next runnel, then expose themselves as they crossed the next bar until they reached the shore. Or, if the landing craft stopped on a bar and allowed the troops to disembark into a runnel, the men might drown under the weight of their equipment, depending upon the depth of the runnel. INTELLIGENCE DIVISION, OFFICE OF THE CHIEF ENGINEER, ETO, US ARMY

Above: Vehicles can be seen moving off the beach in this June 6 photo. Notice the lines of bars and runnels and the beach obstacles now exposed by the low tide. At high tide, the waterline would move up to the seawall, raising the water level by more than 20 feet. NARA/USAAF A-62605AC

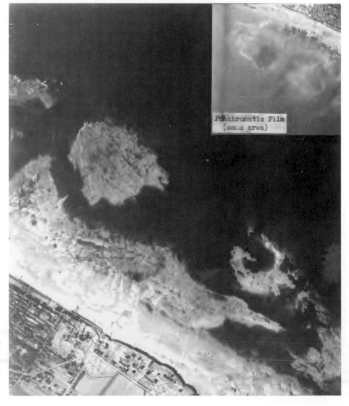

Right: Two photos of the same stretch of beach—one shot with normal, panchromatic film and the other with infrared film—taken on March 24, 1944. The inset image shows particulate clouds in the water, gathering over what can be assumed are underwater features. The main, infrared image sees through the water and gives a clearer picture of the bottom topography. Infrared light is absorbed by water; thus, these photos were taken at a period of very low tide. INTELLIGENCE DIVISION, OFFICE OF THE CHIEF ENGINEER, ETO, US ARMY

HEADING OUT

Above: A jeep from a medical unit drives up the bow ramp of an LCT in preparation for the cross-Channel attack. NARA 111-SC-1209

Left: Troops from the 1st Infantry Division ("The Big Red One") mill about before boarding an LST. Note that the 6 × 6 CCKW truck (C = 1941, C = conventional cab, K = all-wheel drive, W = dual rear axles), commonly referred to as a "deuce-and-a-half" in reference to its 2.5-ton capacity, wears the name *SNAFU* on the front of the hood. *LST-134*, seen in the background, was commissioned on December 7, 1943, under the command of Lt. Edgar G. Curtin (USNR). The ship was immediately sent to the European Theater and participated in the invasions of Normandy and southern France. She was subsequently transferred to the Pacific Theater and supported the assault and occupation of Okinawa and the occupation of Japan. *LST-134* earned three battle stars for her service. NARA 111-SC-1247

Left: US troops line up to board landing craft that will transport them to larger troop-ships waiting outside this English harbor. From the troopships, the soldiers will land on occupied French beaches in the Normandy region. Notice the barrage balloons partially inflated on the dock in the background. NARA 111-SC-1232

Left: Medics and stretcher-bearers file onto an LCT for the 100-mile crossing of the English Channel between Southampton and the Normandy beaches. At 5:17 p.m. local time on June 7, *LCT-653* (seen in the background) was tied up to *LST-157* to take on a load of vehicles to be transferred to Omaha's Easy Red Beach. Shortly thereafter, a DUKW hailed the LST to see if she could accept six wounded soldiers. The LST's medics could care for the soldiers and instructed the DUKW to drive up *LCT-653*'s ramp to unload the wounded and transfer them to the LST. At 5:54 p.m., *LCT-653* cast off and delivered its vehicles to the beach. NARA 111-SC-1248

Below: An LST manned by a US Coast Guard crew prepares to depart England for the Normandy beachhead later in the day on June 6. Note the barge tied up on the port side. World War II censors have allowed the radar antenna to be shown. Many of the vehicles have the US star on top for identification by Allied aircraft, which will have air superiority over the invasion beaches. NHHC/US COAST GUARD 26-G-2358

Facing page bottom: Soldiers and sailors onboard an LCT wait for the signal to move out. The harbor beyond is packed with ships and landing craft of all sizes. NARA 111-SC-1219

Right: Religious services conducted onboard ships while heading across the English Channel were well attended. This service is taking place belowdecks in the troop compartment of an LCI(L). NHHC/US COAST GUARD 26-G-2407

Their uniforms crisp and clean, soldiers from the 101st Airborne Division crowd the deck of an LCT for the trip across the English Channel to France. When an accounting of the D-Day invasion was done in August 1944, the 101st Airborne Division logged 1,240 casualties (182 killed, 557 wounded, and 501 missing) and the accompanying 82nd Airborne Division suffered 1,259 casualties (156 killed, 347 wounded, and 756 missing). NHHC/US NAVY 80-G-59422

SUPREME HEADQUARTERS
ALLIED EXPEDITIONARY FORCE

Soldiers, Sailors and Airmen of the Allied Expeditionary Force!

You are about to embark upon the Great Crusade, toward which we have striven these many months. The eyes of the world are upon you. The hopes and prayers of liberty-loving people everywhere march with you. In company with our brave Allies and brothers-in-arms on other Fronts, you will bring about the destruction of the German war machine, the elimination of Nazi tyranny over the oppressed peoples of Europe, and security for ourselves in a free world.

Your task will not be an easy one. Your enemy is well trained, well equipped and battle-hardened. He will fight savagely.

But this is the year 1944! Much has happened since the Nazi triumphs of 1940-41. The United Nations have inflicted upon the Germans great defeats, in open battle, man-to-man. Our air offensive has seriously reduced their strength in the air and their capacity to wage war on the ground. Our Home Fronts have given us an overwhelming superiority in weapons and munitions of war, and placed at our disposal great reserves of trained fighting men. The tide has turned! The free men of the world are marching together to Victory!

I have full confidence in your courage, devotion to duty and skill in battle. We will accept nothing less than full Victory!

Good Luck! And let us all beseech the blessing of Almighty God upon this great and noble undertaking.

Dwight D Eisenhower

Supreme Allied Commander Gen. Dwight D. Eisenhower circulated this message to Allied forces on the morning of June 6. Eisenhower's words were intended to rally the troops to victory, but everyone knew it would be a long and bloody fight: "Your task will not be an easy one. Your enemy is well trained, well equipped and battle-hardened. He will fight savagely." NARA/THE DWIGHT D. EISENHOWER LIBRARY

CHAPTER ONE

Tactical Operations and the Aerial Invasion

The Germans firmly believed that the Allies would invade the European continent at the narrowest part of the English Channel, between Dover and Calais. The straight-line distance of approximately 26 miles (41.5 km) made sense; however, the Calais area was extensively fortified, and those defenses included eight guns of 200mm or larger plus an additional ten guns ranging between 305mm and 406mm. No invasion fleet could approach this area of the coast, and even the coastal town of Dover was within shelling range of these massive weapons.

To reinforce the belief that the invasion would come in the Calais area, the Allies executed a complex yet convincing deception plan. The overarching plan was known as Operation Bodyguard, and designed to convince the Germans that France and Norway would be invaded simultaneously. The nonexistent British Fourth Army was scripted for the invasion of Norway, and Gen. George S. Patton was given command of the also nonexistent US First Army Group. Allied air superiority denied the Germans the ability to observe military activities in the Fourth Army and US First Army Group's area, so they had to collect intelligence by monitoring radio traffic, news reports, and other information, which was broadcast specifically for consumption by the information-hungry German Army.

In the dark hours on the night of June 5/6, subordinate activities of Operation Bodyguard were launched on and over the English Channel. Facing Calais, Operations Glimmer and Taxable were used to confuse German ship and aircraft radar by presenting what looked like large fleets of ships and aircraft approaching the French coast. Although the targets appeared to be getting closer and closer, they never physically appeared. Operation Mandrel saw the Allies flying bombers working in concert with ships jamming German radar, essentially making the Germans blind to the invasion activities. Operation Titanic saw the Royal Air Force drop 500 dummy parachutists far behind German lines to confuse them as to where the attack was actually occurring and to make the attacking force seem much stronger than it was. The deception operations provided cover for airborne troops that were to drop behind the invasion beaches to secure vital bridges and roadways, and kept German reinforcements at bay until a beachhead could be secured.

THE AERIAL ASSAULT

Shortly after midnight on June 5/6, pathfinder troops parachuted behind German lines to mark drop zones for the first wave of Allied paratroopers. Operation Tonga saw the British 6th Airborne Division drop to the east of the invasion beaches and capture vital bridges crossing the Caen Canal and River Orne. These troops landed near Ranville (Drop Zone N), Varaville (Drop Zone V), and Cuverville (Drop Zone K). They would

be reinforced by glider-borne troops that landed near Le Port (Landing Zone W).

Simultaneously, more than 800 C-47s and C-53s of the IX Troop Carrier Command's 50th, 52nd, and 53rd Troop Carrier Wings shuttled more than 13,100 paratroopers from the American 82nd and 101st Airborne Divisions to 8 drop zones north of Carentan at the base of the Cotentin Peninsula. These drop zones were behind the Omaha and Utah invasion beaches. Low clouds, German antiaircraft fire, small arms fire, and navigation errors all combined to scatter many of the paradrops. Two C-47s dropped their paratroopers directly over Sainte-Mère-Église, where German soldiers shot them dead as they descended in their parachutes or got hung up in trees.

While the Allied paratroopers consolidated their positions, reinforcements and mobile equipment were brought across the English Channel in a massive glider-borne operation. Royal Air Force Hamilcar gliders brought M-22 Locust light tanks, while tricycle-gear Horsa and American CG-4A Hadrian gliders flew in jeeps, mortars, 75mm howitzers, antitank guns, ammunition, food, and reinforcement troops.

Commonwealth troops were tasked with silencing the Merville battery, which was thought to contain four 150mm guns.

Drop Zones, June 6, 1944	
Drop Zone	Nearest Location
101st Airborne Division	
A	Saint-Martin-de-Varreville
C	Hiesville
D	Angoville-au-Plain
E	Hiesville
82nd Airborne Division	
N	Picauville
O	Sainte-Mère-Église
T	Amfreville
W	Les Forges

IX Troop Carrier Command		
50th Troop Carrier Wing, Cottesmore		
439th TCG, Station 462, Upottery		
91st TCS	C-47	fuselage code L4
92nd TCS	C-47	J8
93rd TCS	C-47	3B
94th TCS	C-47	D8
440th TCG, Station 463, Exeter		
95th TCS	C-47	9X
96th TCS	C-47	6Z
97th TCS	C-47	W6
98th TCS	C-47	8Y
441st TCG, Station 464, Merryfield		
99th TCS	C-47	3J
100th TCS	C-47	6B
301st TCS	C-47	Z4
302nd TCS	C-47	2L
442nd TCG, Station 488, Fulbeck		
303rd TCS	C-47	J7
304th TCS	C-47	V4
305th TCS	C-47	4J
306th TCS	C-47	7H
52nd Troop Carrier Wing, Cottesmore		
61st TCG, Station 483, Barkston Heath		
14th TCS	C-47	3I
15th TCS	C-47	Y9
53rd TCS	C-47	3A
59th TCS	C-47	X5
313th TCG, Station 484, Folkingham		
29th TCS	C-47	5X
47th TCS	C-47	N3
48th TCS	C-47	Z7
49th TCS	C-47	H2
314th TCG, Station 538, Saltby		
32nd TCS	C-47	S2
50th TCS	C-47	2R
61st TCS	C-47	Q9
62nd TCS	C-47	E5

315th TCG, Station 493, Spanhoe		
34th TCS	C-47	NM
43rd TCS	C-47	US
309th TCS	C-47	M6
310th TCS	C-47	4A
316th TCG, Station 489, Cottesmore		
36th TCS	C-47	4C
37th TCS	C-47	W7
44th TCS	C-47	6E
45th TCS	C-47	T3
53rd Troop Carrier Wing, Greenham Common		
434th TCG, Station 467, Aldermaston		
71st TCS	C-47	CJ
72nd TCS	C-47	CU
73rd TCS	C-47	CN
74th TCS	C-47	ID
435th TCG, Station 474, Welford Park		
75th TCS	C-47	CK
76th TCS	C-47	CW
77th TCS	C-47	IB
78th TCS	C-47	CM
436th TCG, Station 466, Membury		
79th TCS	C-47	S6
80th TCS	C-47	7D
81st TCS	C-47	U5
82nd TCS	C-47	3D
437th TCG, Station 49, Ramsbury		
83rd TCS	C-47	T2
84th TCS	C-47	Z8
85th TCS	C-47	9O
86th TCS	C-47	5K
438th TCG, Station 486, Greenham Common		
87th TCS	C-47	3X
88th TCS	C-47	M2
89th TCS	C-47	4U
90th TCS	C-47	Q7

Glider Missions, June 6, 1944					
Mission	Departure Airfield	Group	Gliders	Landing Zone	Airborne Div.
Detroit	Ramsbury	437th	52 CG-4A	O	82nd
Elmira	Ramsbury	437th	8 CG-4A, 18 Horsa	W	82nd
	Greenham Common	437th	14 CG-4A, 36 Horsa	W	82nd
	Membury	436th	2 CG-4A, 48 Horsa	W	82nd
	Welford Park	435th	12 CG-4A, 38 Horsa	W	82nd
Chicago	Aldermaston	434th	52 CG-4A	E	101st
Keokuk	Aldermaston	434th	32 Horsa	E	101st
Glider Missions, June 7, 1944					
Galveston	Ramsbury	437th	32 CG-4A, 18 Horsa	W	82nd
	Aldermaston	434th	50 CG-4A	W	82nd
Hackensack	Upottery	439th	20 CG-4A, 30 Horsa	W	82nd
	Merryfield	441st	50 CG-4A	W	82nd

These guns had a range of nearly 2 miles and could reach out to strike Allied ships of the invasion fleet as they approached the beach. The plan called for 600 men of the 6th Airborne Division's 3rd Parachute Brigade to land and advance on the battery. The troops were scattered, however, and only 150 men were able to attack. After capturing the battery, they determined that the four guns were smaller, only 100mm. British paratroopers disabled two of the guns, which cost them half their attacking force (seventy-five men). When the British moved on to the next objective, the Germans recaptured the site, using the remaining two guns against the Allies. The Germans maintained control of the battery until August 17, when the site was abandoned.

One of the first successes of the operation was the capture of the Bénouville Bridge, later to become known as the Pegasus Bridge, and the Orne River Bridge, later remembered as the Horsa Bridge. Landing within yards of the bridges, RAF parachutists and glider-borne troops from the Oxfordshire and Buckinghamshire Light Infantry teamed up with a group of Royal Engineers to capture and, in the face of strong German counterattacks, hold both bridges until later relieved.

Glider missions Chicago and Detroit followed the paratroopers into Normandy before sunrise bringing heavy weapons and additional troops. The Chicago gliders brought men from the 101st Airborne Division, while the Detroit gliders carried men from the 82nd Airborne Division. Later in the evening of June 6, 208 C-47s towed gliders in support of missions Elmira and Keokuk, further reinforcing American troops.

AIR SUPERIORITY STRANGLES ALL MOVEMENT

While the invasion fleet approached the beach at sunrise, Allied fighters patrolled the skies, keeping the Luftwaffe at bay. US Army Air Forces P-47 Thunderbolts and Royal Air Force Typhoons strafed or rocket-attacked any German vehicle that moved or any identifiable enemy strongpoint. Marauding Allied fighters prevented the German Army from moving reinforcements during daylight hours, enabling US and Commonwealth troops to expand the beachhead and move inland.

There were more than 150 German radar sites of all types along the Atlantic Wall, between France's Bay of Biscay and the coast of Norway. Typhoons,

Thunderbolts, and A-20 and B-26 medium bombers paid close attention to these high-priority targets.

Eighth and Fifteenth Air Force B-17 Flying Fortress and B-24 Liberator heavy strategic bombers were employed in a tactical role in the months leading up to and following the invasion. Tactical locations such as railroad marshalling yards, bridges, and coastal defense artillery sites were on the bombers' target list. Each plane could carry a bombload of approximately 8,000 pounds (3,600 kg) on short-range missions. At this stage of the war, the US Army Air Forces and the Royal Air Force could each put up nearly 1,000 heavy bombers per mission. On the night of June 5/6, Royal Air Force Bomber Command sent 1,012 heavy bombers to attack 10 German coastal artillery batteries, scoring a number of direct hits and reducing the enemy's defensive capabilities.

FUEL FOR AN ADVANCING ARMY

In addition to ammunition and food, the Allied armies required vast quantities of gasoline. To deliver needed supplies, Operation Pluto (Pipe Line under the Ocean) had been conceived to flow fuel from England to France using 3-inch-diameter flexible pipes. To move the gasoline, four pipes were laid from the Isle of Wight to Cherbourg (two Hartley-Anglo-Iranian-Siemens pipes, known as HAIS pipes, and two Hamel steel pipes) and sixteen pipes (eleven HAIS and six Hamel) were laid from Dungeness, England, to Boulogne. Operation Pluto delivered 172 million gallons of gasoline between September 1944 and VE Day (May 8, 1945).

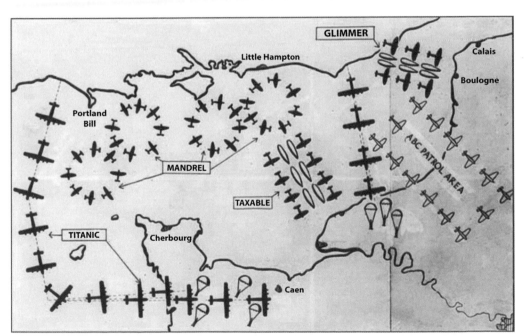

Drawing representing the radar and radio countermeasures that were part of Operation Bodyguard during the early-morning hours of D-Day. While paratroopers and glider-borne infantry would come across the Channel to the south of Cherbourg, Operations Glimmer and Taxable would be used as diversions to mislead the German defenders. Operation Mandrel involved the use of ships along with four B-17 bombers fitted with AN/APT-3 low-frequency radar jammers. Operation Titanic saw the Royal Air Force drop masses of dummy paratroopers with a number of Special Air Service men to create confusion and give the Germans the impression that the invasion force was much larger than it actually was. NARA

Royal Air Force Short Stirling bombers from No. 218 Squadron flew sorties in support of Operation Glimmer. This involved tricking German radar at the Pas-de-Calais into seeing radar returns of a large aerial armada approaching. In addition to the aerial element of Operation Glimmer, six small boats towed radar reflector balloons and transponders that simulated radio traffic among a large fleet of ships. This deception kept the Germans thinking the invasion would materialize where they mistakenly thought it would. KEV DARLING COLLECTION

Operation Taxable involved eighteen small boats accompanied by No. 617 Dam Busters Squadron Avro Lancasters duplicating the tactics of Operation Glimmer, this time to convince the Germans that an invasion force was moving toward La Poterie-Cap-d'Antifer. Here King George VI inspects members of the Dambusters Squadron after their successful breaching of the Möhne and Eder Dams in the Ruhr River Valley of Germany. KEV DARLING COLLECTION

Men of the 101st Airborne Division on the ramp at USAAF Station 463, Exeter, England, on the evening of June 5. They will soon receive the signal to gear up and board the Skytrain for the flight to Normandy. The 101st Airborne was assigned Drop Zones A (at Saint-Martin-de-Varreville) and C (Hiesville) to secure and hold the beach exits for the landing troops as well as to destroy the casemated 88mm guns at Saint-Martin-de-Varreville. At Drop Zone D (Angoville-au-Plain), the 101st was to destroy the bridges across the Douve River and capture the La Barquette lock.

Built at the Douglas Aircraft Company's Oklahoma City factory, C-47-10, serial number 42-92717, was delivered on February 16, 1944, and had flown to England by April 14. This Skytrain survived the war. NARA/US ARMY AIR FORCES

Cpl. Joe E. Oleskiewicz from the 101st Airborne Division strikes a pose in the troop door of a C-47. Oleskiewicz is cradling an M1 Thompson 0.45-caliber submachine gun and has jump goggles around his neck. Face paint was worn by many paratroopers to reduce the reflectivity of their faces. This Skytrain will drop parapacks of equipment (seen under the fuselage) along with paratroopers.
NARA/USAAF 51885AC

Paratroopers stand for inspection before boarding 95th Troop Carrier Squadron C-47A-80-DL, serial number 43-15087. These men will soon fly from Station 463, RAF Exeter, to jump in the dark over enemy territory. Evidence that the invasion stripes were hastily painted on aircraft is evident around the star-and-bar insignia. Paint runs nearly obscure the aft bar. NARA/USAAF 51876AC

A wartime censor has scratched out the 101st Airborne Division shoulder patch of the soldier on the left. The soldier on the right is holding a bazooka. Note that these men are carrying nearly their own weight in equipment and ammunition. Each wears a Mae West inflatable life vest under his parachute harness. NARA/USAAF 52024AC

A Thompson submachine gun–toting paratrooper boards a Skytrain for the cross-Channel attack. Weighed down with gear, most men needed a boost to ascend the ladder into the aircraft. LIBRARY OF CONGRESS

Onboard a Skytrain or Skytrooper, a 101st Airborne noncommissioned officer reads a telegram containing Supreme Allied Commander General Eisenhower's "You are about to embark upon the Great Crusade" message. Allied paratroopers landed in Normandy five hours before the seaborne assault began. NARA/USAAF 53302AC

The training is complete. Spirits are high, and these American paratroopers are ready to drop into occupied France as the leading elements of the invasion. Two of the transport's flight crew have come aft for the photo. Ahead of the bulkhead sits the pilot, copilot, navigator, and radio operator. NARA/USAAF 75891AC

Facing page top: Douglas C-47A-90-DL Skytrain, serial number 43-15665, from the 53rd Troop Carrier Wing, 434th Troop Carrier Group, 73rd Troop Carrier Squadron (fuselage code CN-P), based at Aldermaston, en route to a drop zone in France carrying supplies for Allied troops in parapacks under the wing center section. The parapacks were attached to the underside of the aircraft with bomb shackles. NARA/USAAF 82575AC

Facing page bottom: Douglas C-47s of the 53rd Troop Carrier Wing, 436th Troop Carrier Group's 76th Troop Carrier Squadron (fuselage code CW), based at Welford Park, en route to drop members of the 82nd Airborne Division. The 82nd Airborne landed in Drop Zones N (near Picauville) to destroy additional bridges across the Douve River, O (seizing the town of Sainte-Mère-Église), and T (Amfreville) to help hold the La Fiere causeway. NARA/USAAF 116001AC

Parapacks (A-4 and A-5 delivery containers) dropped to Allied troops during D-Day litter a field. Parapacks typically consisted of equipment that was too heavy to be carried down by paratroopers, such as rations, grenades, rifle and mortar ammunition, and machine guns, and weighed between 210 and 230 pounds each. An M1A1 75mm Pack Howitzer and its M8 gun carriage could be broken down into nine parapacks (Paracrates M1–M7, Parachest M8, and Paracaisson M9). Each was fitted with a 24-foot-diameter cargo parachute of a different color, enabling men on the ground to identify the contents of each parapack without having to open it. Paracrates M1–M5 and M9 were suspended and dropped from under the aircraft, while paracrates M6–M8 were pushed out the cargo door, with the parachutes opening by static cord. Some of the howitzer parapacks could weigh up to 330 pounds.

NARA/USAAF 51675AC

Top: A Troop Carrier Command C-47 floats in the English Channel while a British motorboat stands off. Flying low to drop paratroopers or release gliders exposed the C-47 Skytrains and C-53 Skytroopers to small arms and antiaircraft fire. NARA/USAAF 51617AC

Bottom: Antiaircraft gunners watch the sky in the hours after the initial drops. They are manning an M45 Quadmount (four heavy-barrel 0.50-caliber M2HB Browning machine guns) in an M16 antiaircraft half-track on the perimeter of Station 486, RAF Greenham Common. Each gun was provided with 200 rounds in ammo cans and could put lead downrange at 450–550 rounds per minute. Note the sandbagging around the half-track. In the background are C-47s from the 89th (fuselage code 4U) and 90th (Q7) Troop Carrier Squadrons parked among Horsa gliders. NARA/USAAF 53924AC

GLIDER OPERATIONS

Facing page both: The "Arsenal of Democracy" (Detroit) built 13,903 Waco CG-4 Hadrian gliders during the war. In the months leading up to D-Day, thousands were shipped, disassembled, and crated across the Atlantic to England.

Crookham Common was a large, open field area located east of USAAF Station 486, RAF Greenham Common, open and suitable as a glider assembly depot. Glider fuselages arrived in five crates—cargo section, cockpit, inner and outer wing sections, and tail assembly—and were assembled then towed to the Greenham Common Airfield to be disbursed to the various Troop Carrier Group bases. Crated gliders can be seen in the lower area, with completed fuselages above. Progressing in the assembly process, the inner wing sections were added next, followed by the outboard panels. Note the bivouac area of Army tents at the top of the photo. NARA/USAAF 51194AC AND 52911AC

Top: Ninth Air Force Service Command mechanics attach the port wing to a CG-4A glider. The serial number has been obscured by wartime censors. NARA/USAAF C-51552

Bottom: CG-4A 42-77451 sits at RAF Upottery in East Devon, home to the 50th Troop Carrier Wing's 439th Troop Carrier Group. Sixteen companies built more than 13,000 CG-4As during the war, and this example is one of the 3,190 built by the Ford Motor Company at Kingsford, Michigan. The Kingsford plant employed 4,500 in 3 shifts of 1,500 workers each, building 8 gliders per 24-hour day. NARA/USAAF 75950AC

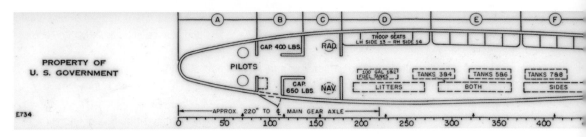

Above: The Douglas C-47 Skytrain was the most versatile cargo aircraft of World War II, with more than 10,000 produced at 3 factories: Long Beach and Santa Monica, California, and Oklahoma City, Oklahoma. The aircraft's reinforced floor and portside double loading doors enabled the interior to be configured to tow gliders, drop paratroopers, carry litter patients and ambulatory wounded, or haul combat equipment such as jeeps, trailers, 37mm antitank guns, or 75mm howitzers. This plan view of the C-47 is from the load adjuster slide rule. Each aircraft carried a load adjuster to calculate the center of gravity before takeoff. Everything loaded onto the aircraft and its position within the fuselage had to be accounted for when figuring the center of gravity. AUTHOR'S COLLECTION

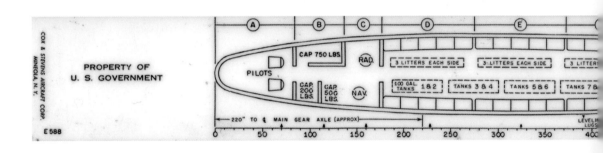

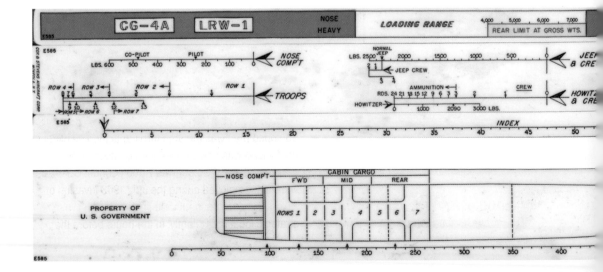

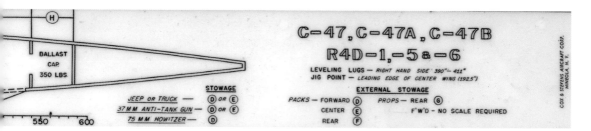

Below: The Douglas C-53 Skytrooper was used to drop paratroopers or two gliders during the aerial invasion and, when a foothold was secured on the continent, to evacuate the wounded back to hospitals in England. These aircraft were built at the company's Santa Monica, California, factory and were very similar to many airline-configured DC-3s delivered before the war.

The C-53 had seating along each side of the cabin for twenty-eight fully equipped troops and was equipped with a single door on the port side. External parapacks could be carried under the fuselage at sections D and E. The C-49 and C-50 were the military designation for the Douglas Sleeper Transport and other early DC-3 airliners impressed into military service. The performance of these former airliners was essentially the same as the C-53. AUTHOR'S COLLECTION

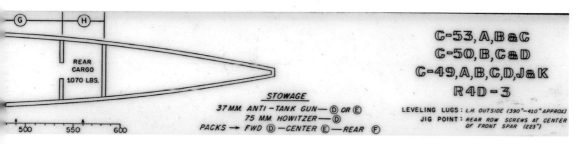

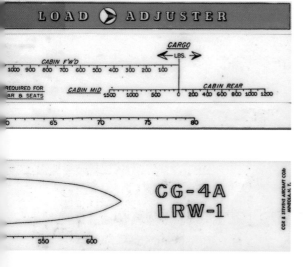

Left: The American Army's choice for a transport glider was the CG-4A Hadrian. The Hadrian featured a fabric-covered tubular steel and wood frame with fabric-covered wooden wings. The cockpit section was hinged, swinging upward to enable a jeep, quarter-ton truck, or 75mm howitzer to be loaded straight-in. When carrying troops, thirteen fully equipped men was the standard capacity. The glider's useful load was approximately 4,200 pounds, and its maximum takeoff weight was 7,500 pounds. CG-4As were first employed during the July 1943 invasion of Sicily and played a major role in deploying troops to strategic locations, silently, in the hours before the D-Day invasion. AUTHOR'S COLLECTION

Men from the 82nd Airborne Division secure a howitzer to the deck of a CG-4A glider. When carrying this type of load, the CG-4A had a useful load of 4,200 pounds (1,905 kg): a crew of two, three passengers, one howitzer, and eighteen rounds of ammunition. NARA/USAAF A-54671AC

Facing page: A trailer is loaded into a Waco CG-4A glider by men from the 82nd Airborne Division. The trailer has a number of stretchers protruding from under the tarpaulin cover. Note the hurriedly painted number on the fuselage. A Horsa glider and a pair of C-47s are parked in the background. NARA/USAAF 54671AC AND 75901AC

Facing page top: CG-4As (left) and Horsa gliders await towplanes as part of the June 7 glider mission Galveston. This photo was most likely taken at USAAF Station 469, RAF Ramsbury, in Wiltshire. The 1st Battalion of the 82nd Airborne's 325th Glider Infantry Regiment, loaded into thirty-two CG-4As and eighteen Horsa gliders at this base, were towed across the Channel and set down at Landing Zone E near Hiesville. Their original destination was Landing Zone W, near Les Forges, but heavy ground fire necessitated the change. Mission Galveston was composed of 100 tug/glider combinations, with the balance of the troops coming across in 50 CG-4As launched from USAAF Station 467, RAF Aldermaston. NARA/USAAF 53243AC

Below: C-47s and Horsa gliders in takeoff position for the D-Day offensive line the runway at RAF Aldermaston in Berkshire. The C-47s are from the 434th Troop Carrier Group's 72nd (fuselage code CU) and 73rd (CN) Troop Carrier Squadrons, which, together with the 71st and 74th Troop Carrier Squadrons, towed thirty-two Horsa and fifty-two CG-4A Hadrian gliders into battle on D-Day. NARA/USAAF 53041AC

Royal Air Force Horsa gliders await the call to duty on the morning of June 6. The American CG-4A gliders were low to the ground, with a tail dragger landing gear configuration and an upswinging nose that enabled straight-in loading of jeeps, trailers, guns, and cargo. The RAF Airspeed Horsa gliders featured tricycle landing gear and a large cargo door on the port side behind the cockpit. This door was large enough to accommodate a jeep, and upon landing, the tail section could be separated from the main fuselage by the removal of eight bolts and some safety wire, enabling jeeps to drive out on ramps carried onboard. NARA/USAAF A-83081AC

Maintainers from the 91st Troop Carrier Squadron at USAAF Station 462, RAF Upottery, prepare a tow rig from the CG-4A glider at left to a C-47 Skytrain. Based on the weather and the lack of invasion stripes, this photo appears to have been taken in late May 1944. NARA/USAAF

Officers from the 439th Troop Carrier Group inspect the tow lug on a C-47 Skytrain. Nearing the landing zone, the glider pilots would uncouple the tow and descend to land, while the Skytrain would drag the tow rope back to base. NARA/USAAF 75738AC

Top: Wearing the shoulder patch of the American 82nd Airborne, these men of the 307th Airborne Medic Company await the signal to board a British Airspeed Horsa glider, RAF serial LJ114. The 307th was part of Mission Elmira, flown on June 6 from RAF Greenham Common by the 438th Troop Carrier Group. When released over Normandy, the gliders of Mission Elmira were to land in Landing Zone W near the villages of Bénouville and Saint-Aubin-d'Arquenay, in the vicinity of the Bénouville Bridge (later to be known as the Pegasus Bridge) over the Caen Canal. NARA/USAAF A15216

Bottom: Skytrains from the 88th Troop Carrier Squadron resume glider tug operations from the runways of USAAF Station 486, RAF Greenham Common, on the evening of June 6. All the Skytrains' engines are turning, and CG-4A number one is about to start the takeoff roll behind a C-47 glider tug. Note how the tow rope connects to the CG-4A at the top of the cockpit frame. NARA/USAAF 83087AC

Facing page top: A C-47 from the 90th Troop Carrier Squadron (fuselage code Q7) departs from Station 486 on June 6. Other Horsas and CG-4As can be seen on the ramp in the distance. NARA/USAAF 51885AC

Facing page bottom: An Airspeed Horsa glider in American markings lifts off behind a C-47 en route to the landing zones in Normandy. Horsas had a long chord and large, thick wings that provided better handling at landing speeds. Unfortunately for the gliders, the trip was usually one way. NARA/USAAF 51742AC

Below: Built at Santa Monica, California, Douglas C-53D 42-68840 is seen towing a CG-4 glider over the English countryside. The C-47/C-53 cargo planes were capable of towing two gliders; however, to keep operations simple, and because there were enough towplanes and crews, they towed only one glider at a time. NARA/USAAF

Ninth Air Force Troop Carrier Command Douglas C-47s tow Waco CG-4A gliders toward the invasion coast. Gliders were a quick way to land reinforcements—both men and equipment—near the battlefront. NARA/USAAF 52479AC

American CG-4A gliders loaded with infantry from the 82nd Airborne are towed by C-47s from the 438th Troop Carrier Group's 88th Troop Carrier Squadron (fuselage code M2). The aircraft pairs launched from RAF Greenham Common on June 6 as part of Mission Elmira and are seen crossing the coast of France. NARA/USAAF 51609AC

LANDED

Towplanes and gliders circle the landing zones later in the day on June 6. Nearly every open field looking into the distance has multiple gliders at one end or another. The fields in the foreground have both CG-4As and Horsas. Most of these landing areas were secure by this time on June 6; however, overflying occupied territory subjected tug- and towplanes to small arms and larger antiaircraft fire. Glider pilots who were released at such low altitudes were essentially committed to land in whatever field, no matter the conditions, lay directly ahead of them, as CG-4As, when fully loaded, had a sink rate of approximately 400 feet per minute. NARA/USAAF 51618AC

Reconnaissance photo from late on June 6 showing a mix of Horsas and CG-4As in French fields. Most look intact, although closer examination shows that a number suffered tragic fates. Wings are missing, and wreckage is strewn about where gliders cartwheeled upon landing or struck rows of trees. A number of Horsas have had their tail sections removed as well. Small groups of white dots are livestock, while evenly spaced dots are obstacles placed by the Germans to defeat landings by gliders. NARA/USAAF 51750AC

Top: Horsa gliders with American markings sit in a French field among parachutes left by airborne infantry; one is still attached to a parapack (near right wing of the top glider). The center and lower-right Horsas have had their tail sections disconnected to allow faster unloading of a jeep or gun. These gliders most likely landed under enemy fire. The Horsa at lower right carries the American star-and-bar insignia on the port wing and the British roundel on the starboard side. NARA/USAAF 52030AC

Bottom: Known as "Rommel's Asparagus," a series of posts were driven into the ground in the fields of Normandy to defeat airborne assault gliders. The idea was to stretch wire between each post to shred the gliders upon contact. This field's asparagus certainly had the better of the CG-4A at left, which has had part of its left outer wing sheared off. Both wings have collapsed, and the cockpit looks to have separated from the fuselage. NARA/US ARMY SIGNAL CORPS

American-marked Horsa glider with cockpit windows shot–up sits in a French pasture following the aerial assault. NARA/USAAF 53206AC

This French field has become a glider graveyard for a pair of CG-4As and the cockpit of a Horsa glider, with another behind it. Waco CG-4A number 11, at left, is likely from glider Mission Chicago, which saw fifty-two C-47s tow CG-4As from Station 467, Aldermaston, across the English Channel. Mission Chicago's aircraft arrived over the Normandy landing zones at 4:00 on the morning of June 6. During this mission 2nd Lt. R. C. Howard, in C-47A-80-DL 43-15101, was forced down by antiaircraft fire and crashed near Étienville. This was his crew's first mission. All five escaped the aircraft and were heading toward Allied lines when they walked into a German ambush. Lieutenant Howard was shot and fell over a shallow bank into a swamp. His crew never saw him again. NARA/USAAF 54016AC

TOP SECRET   ●   ● TOP SECRET

SHAEF
STAFF MESSAGE CONTROL
INCOMING MESSAGE

EYES ONLY

SHAEF CP   SHAEF 83/06

Filed 060800B June   TOR 0609930B June

U R G E N T

FROM : SHAEF COMMAND POST, PERSONAL FROM GENERAL EISENHOWER

TO : AGWAR-TO GENERAL MARSHALL FOR HIS EYES ONLY; SHAEF FOR INFORMATION

REF NO : 90016, 6 June 1944

Local time is now 8 in the morning.

I have as yet no information concerning the actual landings nor of our progress through beach obstacles. Communique will not be issued until we have word that leading ground troops are actually ashore.

All preliminary reports are satisfactory. Airborne formations apparently landed in good order with losses out of approximately 1250 airplanes participating about 30. Preliminary bombings by air went off as scheduled. Navy reports sweeping some mines, but so far as is known channels are clear and operation proceeding as planned. In early morning hours reaction from shore batteries was sufficiently light that some of the naval spotting planes have returned awaiting call.

The weather yesterday which was original date selected was impossible all along the target coast. Today conditions are vastly improved both by sea and air and we have the prospect of at least reasonably favorable weather for the next several days.

Yesterday, I visited British troops about to embark and last night saw a great portion of a United States airborne division just prior to its takeoff. The enthusiasm, toughness and obvious fitness of every single man were high and the light of battle was in their eyes.

I will keep you informed.

DISTRIBUTION:

1. SUPREME COMMANDER ✔

2. CHIEF OF STAFF   DECLASSIFIED

3. SGS   DOD DIR. 5200.10, June 29, 1960

4. Gen. Strong (G-2)   NE by *WGL* date *6-29-67*

5. Gen. Bull (G-3)   TOP SECRET   COPY NO 1
SUPREME COMMANDER

Above: After landing, the men in this Horsa removed the eight bolts attaching the tail section to the fuselage, attached the ramps, and drove out a jeep. The invasion stripes on the underside of the tail show the rush in which they were applied. NARA/USAAF 192609

Left: Memo from General Eisenhower, Supreme Allied Commander, Allied Expeditionary Force (SHAEF), to Gen. George C. Marshall, US Army Chief of Staff, written at 8:00 a.m., June 6, 1944, reporting light losses during the aerial assault and that the operation was proceeding. The decision to delay the invasion by one day is justified by the comment about the favorable weather conditions predicted for the coming days. NARA

NINTH AIR FORCE MEDIUM BOMBERS IN ACTION

During the D-Day landings, this A-20 Havoc from the 410th Bomb Group, 644th Bomb Squadron, based at Gosfield, England, returns from a strike against railyard and oil storage facilities near Carentan. As it passes over the invasion fleet, LSTs can be seen below towing various "rhino ferries," (flat-bottom pontoon barges capable of being driven up, onto the beach to discharge vehicles and supplies), while the LST near the A-20's starboard horizontal tail has a barrage balloon deployed. The 410th Bomb Group put up forty-five planes—a maximum effort for that strike. The group's second strike of the day saw them drop bombs on the railyard near Abbeyville, northeast of Dieppe, part of the Allied plan to keep the Germans thinking the Normandy invasion was just a diversion for the real assault that was to come at Calais. NARA/USAAF 51736AC

Coastal gun emplacements were the D-Day target for the Ninth Air Force's 322nd Bomb Group,
450th Bomb Squadron. Based at USAAF Station 485, RAF Great Sailing, Essex, England, Martin
B-26C-45-MO 42-107685 (fuselage code ER) returns across the English Channel on D-Day. This
Marauder is fitted with "package guns"—four 0.50-caliber machine guns fitted below and behind
the cockpit and fired by the pilot or copilot. The portside guns can be seen in the fairings between
the engine and fuselage. The Ninth Air Force later moved to bases in France, and this aircraft
was transferred to the 387th Bomb Group, 558th Bomb Squadron. It was lost to antiaircraft fire on
February 22, 1945. NARA/USAAF 51590AC

One of many Douglas A-20s leaves a French railroad marshalling yard under a cloud of smoke. This image graphically illustrates the precision with which low-flying medium bombers could strike a target. NARA/USAAF 59176AC

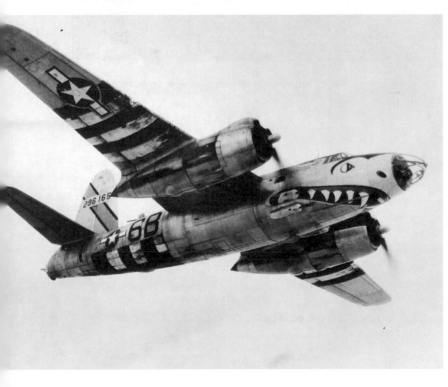

Wickedly painted shark's mouth B-26B-55-MA Marauder, serial number 42-96165, 397th Bomb Group, 599th Bomb Squadron, based at USAAF Station 162 at Chipping Ongar, Essex, England. In June and July 1944, the 39th Bomb Group flew 81 missions with more than 2,000 sorties (one sortie equals 1 aircraft dispatched) with only 1 aircraft lost over enemy territory. The 397th Bomb Group's aircraft were overall bare metal, and 42-96165's shark nose was yellow with red gums around white teeth. NARA/USAAF 55127AC

Douglas A-20 Havocs from the 416th Bomb Group over the cloud-covered coast of France near Le Havre en route to attack rail and transport targets behind Allied lines. In the foreground is A-20G-30, serial number 43-9701, built at Douglas's Santa Monica, California, factory and delivered on December 27, 1943. The aircraft flew from the West Coast to Memphis, Tennessee, to Newark, New Jersey, and from there it was sent to the Eighth Air Force in England (under code SOXO) on January 27, 1944. The Havoc was then assigned to the Ninth Air Force's 416th Bomb Group, 668th Bomb Squadron, at RAF Wethersfield, Essex, England.

Other Havocs lower in the formation wear the fuselage code 5C, denoting their assignment to the 671st Bomb Squadron, also based at RAF Wethersfield. Note that the turret gunners of 5C-K and 5H-Z have their guns facing forward as they scan the sky for the Luftwaffe. This view also shows the rough application of invasion stripes and how quickly they are weathering. NARA/USAAF 52228AC

STRATEGIC BOMBERS AND ALLIED SUPPORT

Photographed from the deck of a PT boat en route to patrol off the invasion beaches, a squadron of B-17 Flying Fortresses passes over at relatively low altitude to strike targets behind enemy lines. B-17 and B-24 strategic bombers were employed tactically alongside the medium bombers of the Ninth Air Force and aircraft from the Royal Air Force to interdict German road and rail traffic in the Normandy region. NHHC NH 44308

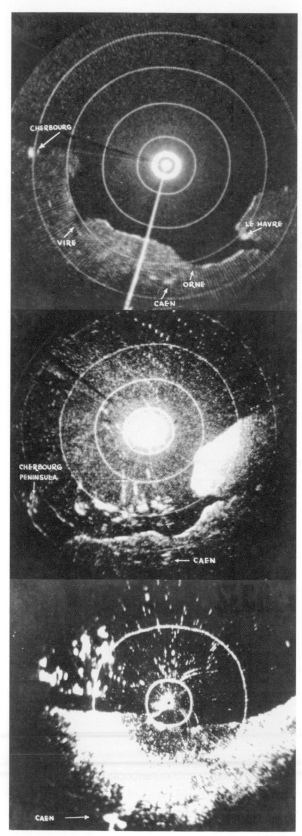

Airborne radar picture of the Bay of the Seine and the Normandy region showing the invasion beaches and large cities, from left, of Cherbourg, Vire, Caen, Orne, and Le Havre. A B-17 fitted with H2X radar in the chin position made this image. H2X was a ground-scanning radar used for bombing when visual aiming techniques were not available due to fog or clouds obscuring the target area. H2X was a development of British H2S radar, and its US technical nomenclature was AN/APS-15 radar. NARA/USAAF 59379AC

The Normandy invasion beaches as seen through an H2X radar screen on the morning of D-Day. The center of the radar picture is approximately 35 miles off the coast and shows the invasion fleet just offshore. NARA/USAAF A-59379AC

The bomber carrying the H2X radar has passed over the invasion fleet and is about to cross the Normandy coast. A trained radar operator was able to distinguish the target from background clutter and drop bombs through overcast. NARA/USAAF B-59379AC

Top: Photo reconnaissance De Havilland DH.98 Mosquitos played a large role in collecting pre- and post-invasion intelligence for Operation Overlord and the subsequent move across France. Mosquito B Mk IX (PR.XVI), RAF serial NS536, was in service with RAF 627 Squadron. The aircraft was written off when its main gear collapsed on landing at Boscombe Down, England, after a navigation exercise on March 13, 1945. WILLIAM T. LARKINS COLLECTION

Bottom: The Royal Air Force's Bristol Beaufighter was extremely lethal with its four forward-firing 20mm cannon. This aircraft, Beaufighter Mk X, RAF serial number JM339, wears invasion stripes and was in the thick of the battle, attacking German shipping. Assigned to RAF 254 Squadron, the aircraft was lost engaging a pair of German M-class minesweepers near Waddenzee Ballumerbocht, the Netherlands, on November 21, 1944. Squadron aircraft attacked the minesweepers, firing twenty-four rockets, with eight striking the ships—one was smoking and the other fully engulfed in flames when last seen. Pilot Sgt. J. Dalley and navigator F/Sgt. G. J. Burns perished in the crash. WILLIAM T. LARKINS COLLECTION

AIR SUPERIORITY STRANGLES ALL MOVEMENT ON THE GROUND

Maintainers gather as an officer gives an update from the front. Note the invasion-striped Lockheed P-38 inside the hangar. NARA/USAAF 52741AC

Lockheed P-38s of the 20th Fighter Group were based at USAAF Station 367, King's Cliffe, Northamptonshire. Prior to D-Day, the 20th Fighter Group received Droopsnoot Lightnings, in which armament in the nose was replaced with a bombardier and a bombsight. The Lightnings would fly a formation similar to the one seen here, and all aircraft would salvo their bombs when they saw the lead aircraft drop. P-38 pilots were not enthusiastic about flying their fighters straight and level on the long bomb run to the target, as they felt they were sitting ducks when bombing for lower altitudes. NARA/USAAF 51937AC

Facing page bottom: P-38J-10-LO 42-68144 (fuselage code 5Y-H) was assigned to the Eighth Air Force's 364th Fighter Group, 384th Fighter Squadron, based at USAAF Station 375, Honington, Suffolk, England. First Lt. William P. Hess's aircraft was damaged in combat and ran off the side of the runway, collapsing the starboard main gear while the engine was making power. The 364th Fighter Group flew 342 missions before transitioning to the North American P-51 Mustang. NARA/USAAF 71931AC

High-back P-51B/Cs of the Eighth Air Force's 361st Fighter Group prepare to take off to escort bombers deep into Germany. The Mustangs carry drop tanks and have been painted with invasion stripes. The stripes helped bomber gunners distinguish the new Mustangs from the German Bf 109s during the heat of combat. NARA/USAAF 52369AC

Mustangs led by Maj. George R. Rew of the Eighth Air Force's 361st Fighter Group, 374th Fighter Squadron, get the takeoff signal to depart USAAF Station 165, RAF Little Walden, Essex, England, shortly after D-Day. These Mustangs are carrying 108-gallon paper drop tanks under each wing. Major Rew is flying P-51B-10-NA 42-106721, *Scarlet Kate*, which was not long for the sky; soon after D-Day he was assigned P-51B-10-NA 42-106763. Rew's new mount was fitted with a Malcolm hood (similar to the canopy on a British Spitfire) and he named his new Mustang *Scarlet Kate II*. That aircraft was lost on a local flight with 2nd Lt. Barry R. Hicks at the controls when its engine quit. Hicks was uninjured in the accident and returned to service. NARA/USAAF 51631AC

Top: Field takeoff control officer 2nd Lt. Jerome R. Mau of Chicago, Illinois, shown launching an Eighth Air Force P-51 Mustang from the 361st Fighter Group's 374th Fighter Squadron. The Mustang shown is P-51B-10-NA 42-106631 (fuselage code E2-K), assigned to Capt. Robert C. Wright. NARA/USAAF 52368AC

Bottom: After escorting bombers to the target, Allied fighters had the option to descend to the deck and strafe targets of opportunity. Here Mustangs wreak havoc on a German airfield somewhere in France. Allied air superiority afforded a great advantage in the breakout from the invasion beaches. NARA/USAAF51467AC

Lt. Gen. James H. "Jimmy" Doolittle looks on as maintainers work on a P-51B at a base in England. Doolittle's Eighth Air Force fighters and bombers provided tactical support to the invasion effort from June 2 to June 17. On D-Day Minus Four (June 2), the Eighth Air Force kept up the diversion by bombing eighteen different targets in the Calais area. Flying 864 heavy bombers into virtually the same airspace took some planning; the area was completely covered by clouds, so bombing would have to be by radar. Escorting the bombers and patrolling to intercept German fighters saw 175 P-47s, 46 P-38s, and 144 P-51s launched as well. On that day, none of General Doolittle's aerial fleet were lost.

NARA/USAAF A-60005AC

Mustangs from the 354th Fighter Group's 356th Fighter Squadron (fuselage code AJ) patrolling over France shortly after D-Day. The 354th was dubbed the "Pioneer Mustang Group," as they were the first American unit to take the new fighter into combat. The group escorted gliders on D-Day, then began strafing targets behind the beaches to prevent German reinforcements from being moved up to meet the invasion force. The group moved to the Allied airfield at Cricqueville (known as A-2) shortly after it opened on June 17. NARA/USAAF 53328AC AND 53328-A

Facing page top: P-51D-10-NA 44-14495 (fuselage code SX-I), *Dallas Doll*, was the personal aircraft of 2nd Lt. Frank H. Bouldin Jr. The Mustang is showing one victory under the cockpit window. Bouldin would finish the war with 3.5 aerial victories. Note the size of the 108-gallon underwing drop tanks. NARA/USAAF 69093AC

Facing page bottom: Col. Thomas J. J. Christian Jr., commanding officer of the 361st Fighter Group, 375th Fighter Squadron, pulls in tight while escorting bombers on a mission in support of the Normandy invasion. Colonel Christian's P-51D-5-NA 44-13410, *Lou IV*, was named for his daughter Lou Ellen. The aircraft also wore the name *Athelene*, thought to be for the wife of crew chief S/Sgt. D. Jameson. Christian's prior aircraft were *Lou* (P-47D-11-RE 42-75494), *Lou II* (P-51B-15-NA 42-106787), and *Lou III* (P-51B-15-NA 42-106942). *Lou IV* and Colonel Christian were lost on August 12, 1944, while strafing the marshalling yard at Boisleux-au-Mont, France. NARA/USAAF 52735AC

P-47D-15-RE 42-76141, *Arkansas Traveler* (LH-Q), was flown by 2nd Lt. Lonnie M. Davis of the 353rd Fighter Group's 350th Fighter Squadron. Davis acquired this aircraft after its former pilot, Capt. Dewey E. Newhart, was killed in action on June 12 flying another aircraft. Newhart had the name *Mud and Mules* painted under the windscreen on the port side. Davis retained the name *Arkansas Traveler* on the starboard side in tribute to his fallen comrade. Note that the checkered squadron markings are also carried on the rudder trim tab. NARA/USAAF 69085AC

In the foreground is invasion stripe–marked P-47D-27-RE 42-27339 heading a lineup of aircraft from the 78th Fighter Group, 82nd Fighter Squadron. Wearing fuselage code MX-S, this is the personal aircraft of then Maj. Joseph E. Myers. Major Myers would share credit for the first aerial victory over an Me 262 jet fighter on August 28, 1944. He was flying 42-27339 during the downing of the jet. Myers retired with the rank of brigadier general in September 1970. Behind Myers's Thunderbolt is Lt. Robert Bosworth's P-47D-22-RE 42-26387, *Miss Behave*, and P-47D-28-REs 44-19846 (MX-W) and 44-19963 (MX-H). NARA/USAAF 55432AC

P-47D-28-RE 44-19898 (fuselage code G9-S) was overall bare metal with a red nose cowl and black rudder band. In the cockpit is Maj. Wayne H. Stout from the Ninth Air Force, 405th Fighter Group's 509 Fighter Squadron. The 405th Fighter Group flew ground attack missions leading up to D-Day. As Allied troops were moving deeper into France, on July 29 the Thunderbolts from the 405th Fighter Group caught a German armored division out in the open on a road outside Avranches, near Mont-Saint-Michel. The column stretched 3 miles (4.8 km) in length; the P-47s knocked out the leading and trailing vehicles, then began to work over all the tanks and trucks trapped in the middle. WILLIAM T. LARKINS COLLECTION

Seen at a forward operating base in France, this invasion stripe–marked P-47D has a pair of 500-pound bombs fitted under the wings. Its eight 0.50-caliber machine guns made it a formidable air-to-air and air-to-ground aircraft. NARA/USAAF 54973AC

P-47D from the 365th Fighter Group's 386th Fighter Squadron on the beach shortly after D-Day. This aircraft is P-47D-15-RE 42-76297, flown by 2nd Lt. John A. Weese. According to 1st Lt. Valmore J. Beaudrault (in "Missing Air Crew Report 5696"): "On June 10, 1944, I led a flight of four on a patrol mission over the Cherbourg assault area. Lieutenant Weese was number four man in my flight. He became separated from the rest of us in the clouds at 1245 hours and 6,000 feet. At 1310 hours he called over the [radio] saying he was hit and his prop was out and his oil pressure was gone. Said he was at 7,000 feet and could see the beachhead and thought he could belly-land behind our lines. He seemed very cool, and I don't think he had been injured."

Weese did indeed ditch his aircraft into the water off the Juno invasion beach at Saint-Aubin-sur-Mer, but he must have been injured by flak, as he was dead by the time rescuers got to his plane. The aircraft was pulled from the water and deposited on the beach.

Saint-Aubin-sur-Mer was within the Juno Beach landing site, where more than 15,000 men of the 3rd Canadian Infantry Division stormed ashore to cut the Caen–Bayeux Road and capture the Carpiquet Airfield. Fighting was fierce, and the airfield was not taken for a month. (NARA/USAAF 72625AC

Fighters from the Eighth and Ninth Air Forces strangled road, rail, and water transportation throughout occupied France in an effort to cut German lines of supply and reinforcement. Here a marshalling yard receives the attentions of marauding Thunderbolts. NARA/USAAF 52397AC

Thunderbolt pilots getting low to destroy aircraft on a German airfield in occupied France. Aside from the dangers of flying too low or being struck by debris from exploding targets, airfield antiaircraft fire was murderous and accounted for more fighter losses in the closing year of the war than did German pilots. NARA/USAAF 51466AC

A German train releases pressure from its boiler as the 0.50-caliber bullets from a P-47 Thunderbolt find their mark. Allied air superiority kept the Germans bottled up during daylight hours. NARA/USAAF 51465AC

German Dornier 217 night fighters come under the guns of a P-47 as the Thunderbolt destroys everything during a low-level strafing pass. Germany's lack of fuel and oil combined with a dedicated campaign to destroy German aircraft, whether the aircraft were on the ground or in the air, enabled Allied troops to move across occupied France with minimal threat of attack from the sky. NARA/USAAF 55186AC

Still frame from a Thunderbolt's gun camera showing the destruction of a German aircraft, most likely an Arado Ar 96 tandem-seat trainer. The trainer's wing tank has caught fire, and the aircraft is not long for the sky. NARA/USAAF 56871AC

CHAPTER TWO

Operation Neptune: Hit the Beach!

Having crossed the English Channel, the largest naval force assembled to date filled the Bay of the Seine off the Normandy coast. The bay stretches 62 miles (100 km) from the Cotentin Peninsula in the west to the city of Le Havre at the Seine estuary on the east. Within the Bay of the Seine, the majority of the Allies' invasion vessels began arriving on the morning of June 6, at approximately 5:00 a.m. to begin the assault on the Normandy beaches. By the end of the day, 6,939 vessels had participated in the invasion.

First to reach the Bay of the Seine were minesweepers, arriving in the area near midnight. For the next five hours, these wooden warriors swept channels for the bombardment ships that were soon to arrive. Nearly 350 minesweepers, motor launches, and other support vessels cleared 10 channels, each 400 to 1,200 yards wide, for the amphibious assault forces. They then escorted the big-gun ships of the bombardment force as they steamed into position.

While the amphibious ships were deploying landing craft and preparing to send boats ashore, the guns of the bombardment force opened fire. The Eastern Task Force (British) consisted of battleships HMS *Warspite* and *Ramilles*; cruisers HMS *Ajax, Argonaut, Mauritius,* and *Orion*; monitor HMS *Roberts*; and other ships accompanied by thirty-seven destroyers. The Western Task Force (American) Bombardment Force A consisted of the battleship *Nevada* (BB-36), cruiser *Quincy* (CA-71), monitor HMS *Erebus*, light cruisers HMS *Black Prince* and *Enterprise,* and Dutch gunboat HNLMS *Soemba*, plus six destroyers and twenty-one support craft. Bombardment Force C comprised the battleships *Texas* (BB-35, force flagship) and *Arkansas* (BB-33), cruiser HMS *Glasgow*, and French light cruisers *Georges Leygues* and *Montcalm*, plus twelve destroyers and thirty-seven support craft. The Western Task Force engaged targets at and behind Omaha and Utah Beaches, with *Texas* concentrating her fire on the gun emplacements at Pointe du Hoc.

At 5:05 a.m., the German 210mm (8.25-inch) coastal defense guns at Saint-Marcouf, in the Utah Beach sector, placed the American destroyers *Corry* (DD-463) and *Fitch* (DD-462) under fire. *Corry* engaged the shore battery with her 5-inch guns. At 6:30 a.m., she was struck amidships in the engineering spaces. Her rudder jammed, and she began to circle while taking on water fast. Oddly enough, although her commander, Lt. Cdr. George D. Hoffman, reported that she had been struck by an artillery shell, the official record reflects that she was sunk by a mine. *Fitch* and other ships in the area were able to rescue all but one officer and twenty-two sailors.

ASSAULTING THE BEACH

British, Canadian, Czech, Dutch, Free French, New Zealanders, Norwegian, Polish, and South African soldiers and sailors participated in Operation Neptune and the invasion of Gold, Juno, and Sword Beaches at the eastern end of the Bay of the Seine. On the west end of the bay, American troops went ashore at Omaha and Utah Beaches. The advance up Utah Beach was easy compared to the relatively difficult terrain and withering enemy fire encountered at Omaha Beach. At Utah Beach during D-Day, American forces were able to put 23,250 men ashore along with 1,742 vehicles and 1,695 tons of supplies, with the loss of 197 men.

Omaha Beach was another story. The area had been divided into eight segments (from west to east: Charlie, Dog Green, Dog White, Dog Red, Easy Green, Easy Red, Fox Green, and Fox Red). German strongpoints guarded the beach exits, with the heaviest troop concentrations at Vierville (Charlie and Dog Green), Les Moulins (Dog Red and Easy Green), and Fox Green Beach, which faced two beach exits, one leading to Colleville and the other through the bluffs.

Rough seas swamped a number of landing craft, and a strong current coupled with low visibility pushed many assault boats off course, causing them to come ashore in the wrong area. Pre-invasion bombing had missed many of the German defenses due to poor visibility and the desire not to drop too close to American troops coming ashore. Stiff German resistance kept the invaders pinned down for hours. It was not until a number of tanks were able to gain the beach and begin engaging the defenders at close range that any progress was made.

As the second wave of men came ashore around 7:00 a.m., the tide was coming in, hiding beach obstacles, which in turn damaged or destroyed a large number of landing craft. Rough seas swamped a number of DUKW trucks as they attempted to wade ashore, and the narrow beach caused a traffic jam, forcing the beach master from the 7th Naval Beach Battalion to call a halt to further vehicle landings at 8:30 a.m., until the situation improved.

At 9:00 a.m., gunfire from destroyers offshore and tanks on the beach enabled comingled elements of the 3rd Battalion of the 116th Infantry Regiment (29th Infantry Division) and the 16th Infantry Regiment (1st Infantry Division) to climb the bluff and begin advancing inland from Fox Green Beach.

Down the beach, three companies of the 2nd Ranger Battalion were landing on a narrow strip of beach, preparing to assault the 100-foot-tall cliffs of Pointe du Hoc. Their objective was to destroy six 155mm cannon and remove the

Germans from their high vantage point, which had a commanding view of both Omaha and Utah Beaches. As the Rangers worked their way up, naval gunfire support came from the destroyer *Satterlee* (DD-626), preventing German defenders from firing down on the men climbing up the cliff. *Satterlee* supported the Rangers throughout the day as they held the high ground. The Rangers' objective, the six 155mm guns, had in fact been removed from the top of Pointe du Hoc to an area south of the coastal highway. Five of the guns were located and thermite grenades exploded in the breaches, destroying them.

By the end of the day, the Allies had established a beachhead and begun to move inland.

EMERGENCY INVASION HARBORS

Until the harbor at Cherbourg could be taken, the Allies needed port facilities to efficiently bring men and materiel ashore. To this end, they brought a number of war-weary ships to Normandy, where they purposely sunk them to form artificial breakwaters; these ships were known as "gooseberries." One gooseberry was built to shelter each of the landing beaches: Gooseberry 1 at Utah Beach (ten ships), Gooseberry 2 at Omaha Beach (fifteen ships), Gooseberry 3 at Gold Beach (sixteen ships), Gooseberry 4 at Juno Beach (eleven ships), and Gooseberry 5 at Sword Beach (nine ships).

On the shore side of the ships at Gooseberry 2 and 3, prefabricated concrete caissons, known as "phoenixes," built in England and towed across the Channel, were sunk in position to form a more substantial port facility. The gooseberry and phoenix components formed "mulberry harbors," of which two were constructed: Mulberry A off the shore at Saint-Laurent-sur-Mer (Omaha Beach) and Mulberry B at Arromanches (Gold Beach). Inside the mulberry breakwaters, floating piers with roadways, known as "whales," extended to pier heads, known as "spuds."

Both mulberry harbors were beginning operations when, on June 19, a storm blew in and destroyed Mulberry A at Omaha Beach. Mulberry B, which became known as "Port Winston," after the British prime minister, was damaged in the storm but subsequently repaired. Mulberry A was abandoned, and landing ship tanks (LSTs) were used to supply American forces until September 1944. As the Allies moved across France and Belgium, more permanent port facilities were captured and put to use.

HEADING TO THE BEACH

The forward 14-inch/45-caliber guns of the battleship USS *Nevada* (BB-36) bombard the invasion beaches prior to men landing on Utah Beach on the morning of D-Day. As the troops moved off the beach, *Nevada* and other ships of the fire support task force lobbed shells onto German Army targets inland. The 14-inch (356mm) naval guns onboard *Nevada*, at an elevation of 15 degrees, could fire a 1,400-pound armor-piercing shell 23,000 yards (21,000 meters, or 13.06 miles). Caliber refers to the length of the barrel; thus a 14-inch/45-caliber gun barrel (14-inch diameter × 45 caliber) has a length of 630 inches, or 52.5 feet. With the breech, a 14-inch/45-caliber gun has an overall length of 53 feet, 6.5 inches (16.32 meters).NHHC 80-G-252412

Steaming off Utah Beach, *LCT(R)-48* (Landing Craft Tank [Rocket]-48) is heading to reload its launch racks. Capable of firing more than 1,000 3-inch-diameter, 60-pound (27.2-kg) projectiles, these craft could saturate a beach with explosives in a matter of seconds. The LCT(R) was converted from a standard landing craft tank by sealing the bow door and adding an additional deck for the rocket racks. The space between decks ('tween decks) could hold 5,000 additional rockets. The boat was equipped with a Type 970 radar to give range to the target and for navigation. The Type 970 was an airborne 9-centimeter radar (known as H2X, with the antenna mounted upside down for maritime use).

NHHC 80-G-252483

Facing page: A convoy of LCI(L)s (landing craft infantry [large]) sails toward the D-Day invasion beaches, each with an Mk VI box kite (barrage balloon) deployed against enemy low-level strafers. In the foreground are the decks of the USS *Ancon* (AGC-4), an amphibious force command ship.

Ancon was built as a passenger steamship for the Panama Railroad Company and was launched on September 24, 1938. The US Army acquired the ship shortly after the war broke out, and she was transferred to the US Navy on August 7, 1942. *Ancon* participated in Operation Torch, putting troops ashore at Fedhala, French Morocco. A little less than a year later, *Ancon* served as the flagship for the Omaha Beach invasion.

The bottom photo looks from the bow of *Ancon* toward the invasion beaches, with *LST-373* at right. *LST-373* took part in the Sicilian occupation (July 9–15, 1943) and the Salerno, Italy, landings (September 9–21, 1943), followed by its presence, as shown here, supporting the Normandy landings. In December 1944, *LST-373* was transferred to the Royal Navy and was redesignated HM *LST-373*. She then sailed to the Pacific Theater and supported all major operations, from Rangoon to Malaya, Singapore, and Bangkok. She worked to repatriate Allied POWs before being returned to the US Navy in March 1946. NHHC 80-G-231247 AND 80-G-231248

LCI(L)-217 makes her way across the English Channel with a kite balloon deployed. Eleven LCI(L)s were heavily damaged or sunk during the invasion, with another eighty-three severely damaged. This LCI(L) served the US Navy in support of the occupation of North Africa (March 27–July 9, 1943), then in the invasion of Sicily and operations up the west coast of Italy. After the Normandy campaign, *LCI(L)-217* was transferred to the Royal Navy in November 1944. Following the conclusion of the war, the LCI returned to American ownership on March 14, 1946, and was sold to the French Navy five days later, on March 19. The French renamed her RFS *L9046*. NHHC 80-G-252368

Top: Landing craft—in this case landing craft vehicle personnel (LCVP)—head back to their ship, *LST-284*, after having discharged men and equipment on the invasion beaches. *LST-284* saw service at Normandy and the invasion of southern France before being transferred to the Pacific Theater, where she supported the landings at Okinawa.

LCVPs were designed by Andrew Higgins of Higgins Industries in New Orleans, Louisiana, and more than 23,350 were built by the company and other contractors before the war ended. NHHC 80-G-252687

Bottom: USS *Bayfield* (APA-33) was laid down at Western Pipe and Steel in South San Francisco, California, for the Maritime Commission on November 14, 1942, as SS *Sea Bass*. Launched on February 15, 1943, she was redesignated an attack transport. The ship was transferred from the Maritime Commission to the Navy in June 1943 and was operated by an all–Coast Guard crew. She is seen off the Utah invasion beach, with her LCVPs circling at the stern awaiting reloading while her forward deck cranes lower more boats into the water. An LST, LCI, and LCT can be seen in the background at right. NHHC 80-G-252391

While Allied troops continue to flood ashore on June 8, American senior officers observe landings on the beaches of Normandy from the decks of the cruiser *Augusta* (CA-31). From left: Rear Adm. Alan G. Kirk (US Navy, Commander Western Naval Task Force), Lt. Gen. Omar N. Bradley (US Army, Commanding General, US First Army), Rear Adm. Arthur D. Struble (holding binoculars US Navy, Chief of Staff for Rear Admiral Kirk), and Maj. Gen. Ralph Royce (US Army). NHHC 80-G-252940

Prior to the invasion, US Army and Navy officers gathered to watch units going ashore on the English coast. Standing to the right of Lt. Gen. Omar Bradley is Rear Adm. John L. Hall Jr. (US Navy), who led Amphibious Force O in support of US Army V Corps' assault on Omaha Beach; Maj. Gen. Leonard T. Gerow (US Army), commander of V Corps and the first corps-level commander to land on the European continent on D-Day; and Maj. Gen. Clarence L. Huebner (US Army), commanding officer of the 1st Infantry Division, "The Big Red One," which assaulted Omaha Beach. NHHC 80-G-253483

Top: Lying off Omaha Beach on D-Day, command ship *Ancon* (AGC-4), at right, with submarine chaser *PC-564* slowly making its way toward shore. Headquarters units were dispatched from *Ancon* to the beaches as troops moved inland. NHHC 80-G-257287

Bottom: The US Coast Guard provided sixty 83-foot cutters (83 feet, 2 inches in length, with a beam of 16 feet, 2 inches) to support Operation Neptune. The cutters were assigned to USCG Rescue Flotilla No. 1, based at Poole, England. Each displaced 76 tons, had a maximum speed of 20 knots, and was driven by twin 600-horsepower, eight cylinder in-line Sterling Viking II Model TCG-8 gasoline engines, displacing 3,619.1 cubic inches, which turned twin screws.

While on D-Day patrols, 83-foot cutters rescued 1,437 men and 1 woman. Two of the cutters were lost in the days following the June 6 landings; *USCG-27* (83415) and *USCG-47* (83471) were both lost in a storm on June 21, 1944, after contacting underwater wreckage from the invasion. NARA

Above: The *USCG-1*, formerly the 83300/ex-CG 450, escorted the first waves of landing craft into the Omaha assault area on D-Day morning. The crew of *USCG-1* pulled twenty-eight survivors out of the English Channel from a sunken landing craft right off the beaches before 7:00 a.m. on D-Day. US COAST GUARD HISTORIAN'S OFFICE

Left: The 83-foot Coast Guard cutter *USCG-1* (83300/ex-CG 450) off Omaha Beach on the morning of D-Day, tied up to *LCT (Mark VI)-549* and the attack transport USS *Samuel Chase* (APA-26). *Samuel Chase* was part of Assault Group 0-1, which landed the 1st Division (famous as "The Big Red One") on the Easy Red section of Omaha Beach. US COAST GUARD HISTORIAN'S OFFICE

ASSAULTING THE BEACH

In the waters off Sword and Juno Beaches, two 52-foot-long midget submarines were waiting for the invasion fleet. They were not there to attack. The submarines were Royal Navy X-Class midgets that had departed England, arriving off the invasion beaches on June 1. *X-20* and *X-23* sat on the bottom during the day and surfaced at night to listen to the BBC for the coded message signaling that the invasion was coming the following morning. Early on the morning of June 6, both craft surfaced and hoisted a lighted mast that shone out to sea, essentially acting as lighthouses to aid landing craft in their approach to the beaches. AUTHOR'S COLLECTION

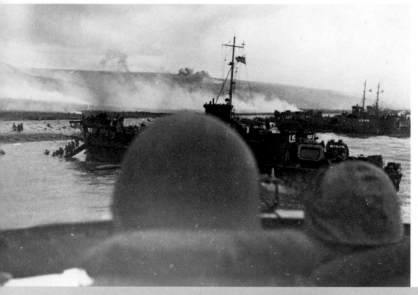

The German Army fought savagely on D-Day, and USS *LCI(L)-553* and USS *LCI(L)-410* are seen disembarking troops from the 16th Regimental Combat Team into the maelstrom on Omaha Beach's Fox Green section. *LCI(L)-553* struck two underwater mines approaching the beach and then was hit by a pair of German 88mm cannon shells. Raked by fire and unable to back her away from the beach, the crew abandoned ship and went ashore. NHHC 80-G-421287 AND 80-G-421288

Top: Action on Omaha Beach as troops wade ashore from *LCI(L)-412*. The rise between the sea and shore provides little cover, but men hunker down as *LCI(L)-412*'s bow gunner engages the enemy with his 20mm cannon. Half-tracks have entered the water behind the soldiers to provide cover fire for their forthcoming advance. NHHC 80-G-421289

Bottom: Soldiers make their way to dry ground, having stepped off the bow ramp of a US Coast Guard–crewed LCVP. Smoke and beach obstacles can be seen in the background. NARA/US COAST GUARD 26-G-2343

Top: Smoke rises from devastated German positions as a rhino ferry, seen at center, brings men and vehicles from the Ninth Air Force's engineers to Omaha Beach. The Engineer Aviation Battalions moved right behind frontline troops to scrape out emergency landing fields from the countryside as well as refueling and rearming strips for fighter-bombers supporting the advance. The rhino ferry was constructed by lashing together pontoons (6 × 6 feet each, then bolted together, six pontoons wide and thirty pontoons long); it was towed across the Channel by an LST and then cut loose as it approached the beachhead. The rhino then drove itself to shore using its twin Chrysler outboard motors. Troops, vehicles, and large amounts of ammunition were typical loads for a rhino ferry. The rhinos could also be tugged across the Channel empty, then used as barges to offload vehicles and supplies from LSTs. They were also used as piers, with an LST docking bow-on, lowering its ramp, and discharging vehicles to travel across the rhino and then onto the beach. NARA/US ARMY 51764AC

Bottom: Aerial photo of the beaches at Grandcamp-les-Bains, France, east of Utah Beach, reveals its anti-invasion obstacles at low tide. Here the Germans used large logs topped with Teller mines to defeat boats approaching the beaches. At high tide, these would be unseen, hiding below the water's surface. NARA/US ARMY 190653

Ninth Air Force B-26 Marauder medium bombers escorted by P-38s, P-47s, and P-51s were over the invasion beaches at first light to attack German positions at the five invasion points. Once the bombers had attacked their targets, the fighters remained to protect the invasion flotilla and attack anything that moved behind the beachhead. NARA/US ARMY 51697 AND 51988

Flagship of the bombardment force in the waters off Omaha Beach, battleship *Texas* (BB-35) turned its 14-inch, 45-caliber guns against Pointe du Hoc, firing 255 shells in 34 minutes. Her secondary 5-inch guns pummeled the beach area exit known as D-1. With Allied troops unable to break the German resistance along Omaha Beach, *Texas* closed to within 3,000 yards of the shore and began firing at nearly point-blank range to help break up German troop concentrations. *Texas* continued her fire support mission until June 8, when she retired to England to refuel and rearm. The battleship was back in action by June 11.

On June 25, *Texas* was again off the coast of France, this time bombarding targets near Cherbourg. In company with battleships *Arkansas* and *Nevada*, the three battlewagons sparred with the four 240mm guns of the Fermanville battery, 6 miles east of Cherbourg. Supporting the battleships were destroyers *Barton* (DD-722), *O'Brien* (DD-725), *Laffey* (DD-724), *Hobson* (DD-464), and *Plunkett* (DD-431). Minesweepers clearing a firing lane ahead of the larger ships were straddled by shells.

Around 12:20 p.m., *Texas* was struck by a 280mm shell, which hit the armored conning tower, killing the helmsman, Quartermaster 3rd Class Christen N. Christensen. Another 280mm shell struck her hull, but this one was a dud. Shortly thereafter, *Texas* knocked out one of the Fermanville battery's four guns. At 3:00 p.m., all the ships retired; the battery was subsequently taken by ground troops on June 29. NHHC NH 63648

Top: Fully loaded with troops from the 1st Infantry Division, *LCI(L)-490* (left) and *LCI(L)-496* approach Omaha Beach on D-Day during the first wave. Gunfire is impacting the beach, but there are few vessels or vehicles ashore at this point. Note the two LCVPs sailing out past the LCIs to pick up another load. ARMY SIGNAL CORPS SC 189987

Bottom: All sorts of landing craft, including LCMs, LCI(L)s, and LCTs, can be seen headed for Omaha Beach during the morning of D-Day. At low tide, men of the 1st Infantry Division had to cover 300 yards of beach from the landing craft to the first ledge. From there, they had another 100 yards to travel before they could gain cover from the terrain. ARMY SIGNAL CORPS SC 189988

Top: Soldiers from the 16th Regimental Combat Team look on from their LCVP as they near Omaha Beach. Mixed in with the LCVPs are DUKW amphibious trucks, and DUKWs can be seen onshore. ARMY SIGNAL CORPS SC189986

Bottom: LCVP from attack transport *Samuel Chase* (APA-26) about to land, with a sailor standing on the ramp. The fact that he's standing in the open indicates this photograph was taken later on D-Day. *LCI(L)-553*, at left, was abandoned hours earlier. The truck at lower right has a sign warning those who will follow that the driver sits on the left side and the vehicle has no turn signals. ARMY SIGNAL CORPS SC189899

Two views of the tremendous number of ships employed during the invasion of just one beach, along with the destruction wrought by shore bombardments and aerial bombing. Hundreds of vehicles can be seen on the sand and along the beach exit roads. NARA/US ARMY 53469AC AND 53519AC

Above: Another view of the Utah Beach area showing vehicles streaming inland from the beach exit. Fires burn houses and former German strongpoints. Of the LSTs grounded in the surf line, the ship at the lower left and parallel to the beach is unloading its cargo of vehicles in the lee of an empty LST. This seemingly odd positioning blocked the incoming surf from impacting vehicles as they drove down the bow ramp and onto the beach. NARA/US ARMY B-62605AC

Facing page top: The low terrain along the Utah Beach sector enabled men and equipment to stream inland once initial German resistance was broken. The volume of men and materiel coming ashore prevented the Germans from repulsing the invasion on the beaches. NARA/US ARMY 51579AC

Facing page bottom: Massive bomb craters can be seen in the foreground as LCIs approach Utah Beach. NARA/US ARMY 52281AC

Above: A mass of vehicles crowd the beach as others move up the roadway to the interior of France. Nearly every square yard of land in the foreground has been marked with a bomb or shell hole, demonstrating the intensity of the pre-invasion bombardment and aerial bombing. NARA/US ARMY 58416AC

Below: US Army vehicles can be seen leaving the beach and heading inland. Note the large amount of beach obstacles on the sand and in the surf line as well as the landing craft attempting to thread their way to the shore. NARA/US ARMY A-62605AC

On the afternoon of D-Day, Ninth Air Force B-26 Marauder medium bombers returned to attack targets behind enemy lines. Bombing at low altitude, the Marauders hit gun positions and troop strongpoints, as well as road and rail targets. This photograph of the Utah Beach area shows hundreds of bomb and shell craters. The road leading away from the beach is filled with Allied vehicles moving inland. NARA/ USAAF 52406AC

Aerial view of the Saint-Laurent-sur-Mer area of Omaha Beach, with the first airstrip (A-21C) visible behind the invasion beach. The chain of Liberty ships in the center of the photo were deliberately sunk to form a breakwater to shelter Omaha Beach. Known as mulberry harbors, they would enable the Allies to supply their troops ashore without having to assault the closest port, which was Cherbourg.

On June 19, a gale-force storm tore apart the mulberry harbors, rendering them useless and making the capture of Cherbourg a priority. Seven days later, Cherbourg fell to the Allies and became an important port throughout the remainder of the war. During their service, mulberry harbors enabled more than 12,000 tons of supplies and more than 2,500 vehicles to come ashore each day. NARA/US ARMY 72990AC

ON THE BEACH

Numerical superiority in men, vehicles, and ships is dramatically illustrated in this photo of the invasion beaches at low tide. Every type of cargo ship can be seen in the background, while more than half a dozen LSTs unload. An LCT is seen high and dry in the center of the photograph, while truck and half-track convoys prepare to depart the beach. Identifiable LSTs are *LST-532* (in the center of the view), *LST-262* (third LST from right), *LST-310* (at right, preparing to launch barrage balloon), *LST-533* (partially visible at far right), and *LST-524*. NARA/US COAST GUARD 26-G-2517

Above: Omaha Beach on the afternoon of D-Day with vehicles and a tank mired in the sand. Note the bodies in the foreground, yet to be collected by Graves Registration troops. NHHC 80-G-45714

Facing page top: Omaha Beach after the siege had been lifted and LSTs were able to swarm ashore. Note the difference between the US- and British-operated LSTs: The Royal Navy ships wear their hull numbers in colored blocks and are painted in striped camouflage, while the American LSTs are painted a dark blue overall (known as Measure 21 camouflage). Identifiable LSTs on the beach are, from right, *LST-312*, British *LST-320* and *LST-321*, *LST-72*, an unidentified US Navy LST, British *LST-324*, *LST-311*, *LST-49*, *LST-373*, *LST-47*, and two more unidentified LSTs. NHHC 80-G-46817

Facing page bottom: During unloading operations on the afternoon following D-Day, an explosion rocked the beach area as engineers destroyed German land mines. British *LCT-996* is at the extreme right, stranded by low tide. British *LCT-799* is alongside, just to the left; several other landing craft are also present. LCTs could carry up to ten tanks. NHHC 80-G-252257

A pair of LCMs approach Utah's Green Beach two days after the invasion. Light can be seen through the roof of the house on the beach as DUKWs roam up and down the surf line. NHHC 80-G-252624

Carrying supplies to shore, an amphibious DUKW, christened *Jesse James*, wades ashore at, most likely, Utah Beach on June 11. Note how the cargo was lowered into the DUKW in nets, which will be retrieved by cranes on the beach. NHHC 80-G-252737

Members of the 9th Service Group, IX Air Service Command, about to go ashore from an LST on Omaha Beach in the days following the invasion. The shallow-draft LSTs could get extremely close to the beach for a vessel of their size. Note the 40mm cannon at the bow and that the LST has dropped anchor. NARA/US ARMY 61288AC

It's all about weight and balance. *LST-325* sits on the beach at low tide with the majority of her weight aft of midships, requiring a sand ramp to be built under her bow doors. The sand ramp enabled vehicles to be offloaded while the tide was out.

LST-325 made forty-three round-trips bringing supplies from England to France in support of Allied troops. She is most noted for the December 28, 1944, rescue of more than 700 men from the Royal Navy infantry landing ship *Empire Javelin* between Southampton, England, and Le Havre, France.

After the war, *LST-325* was transferred to the Greek Navy on May 1, 1964 through the Military Assistance Program. The Greeks renamed her HS *Syros* (L-144) and sailed her for more than thirty years. She is now an operating memorial ship based in Evansville, Indiana (see appendix VI: Select D-Day Survivors). NHHC 80-G-252795

Left: *LST-138* unloads a portable photographic laboratory destined for a Ninth Air Force advance airfield to support the needs of frontline tactical reconnaissance squadrons. A US Army bulldozer pulls the tractor-trailer combination across the soft sand of Omaha Beach. Note that the RAF truck tractor wears the name *Evelyn Ann*. NARA/USAAF 56610AC

Facing page bottom: Tons of supplies are seen sitting on Omaha Beach on June 15, as British LCTs lie parallel to the surf line. British *LCT(A) (5)-2421* is identifiable behind *LCT-555* in the center. *LCVP X-19* in the foreground wears the name *Angela* and *Cincinnati, Ohio*, on her port side. DUKWs can be seen moving cargo among the various LCTs stranded on the beach. NHHC 80-G-252568

Multiple 40mm cannon point skyward on *LST-325* as she and *LST-388* unload at low tide. Note the guard between the rudder and the propellers to keep the spinning blades from contacting the sea floor. Also note the Danforth-style anchor at the stern of *LST-325*. This anchor could be dropped as the LST sailed onto the beach; then, as the tide rose, it could be reeled in, pulling the ship off the beach. NHHC 80-G-252797

Facing page top: Fitted with raised air intakes, M4 Sherman *Cannon Ball* was from the 70th Tank Battalion, which waded ashore at Utah Beach on D-Day. The 70th lost nine of its forty-eight Shermans during the beach assault. *Cannon Ball*, seen here, dropped into an underwater shell hole and had to be abandoned during the invasion. She was later recovered and put back into service. NHHC 80-G-252802

Facing page bottom: Having routed the Germans, a Navy shore battalion moves into their former enemy's slit trenches and bunkers behind the seawall. DUKW amphibious trucks can be seen maneuvering toward the beach exit, while an LCT and other landing craft in the background bring in supplies. NHHC 80-G-252734

Below: Engineers from the US Navy's 2nd Beach Battalion examine a pair of Leichter Ladungsträger Goliath (Sd.Kfz. 302/303a/303b) tracked mines. To the Allies, they were known as "beetles." The beetles were tracked vehicles packed with explosives and were 4 feet long, 2 feet wide, and about 1 foot tall. They were remotely controlled by a wire, and the Germans intended to drive them out to detonate under a landing craft or Allied tanks. Two versions of beetles were built, differing in the size of the explosive (either a 30-pound/66-kg or 220-pound/100-kg charge). These beetles are being dismantled on Utah Beach on June 11. NHHC 80-G-252744

Top: Although sited near Cherbourg and seen after capture by Allied troops on July 3, this concrete gun emplacement was typical of the coastal defenses engaged during the invasion. NHHC 80-G-254307

Bottom: This gun in a German pillbox was destroyed by naval gunfire. Note the shell impact point above the German gun on the edge of the slit. An Allied shell clipped the opening, traveled into the bunker, and exploded, killing the gun crew and silencing the weapon. By June 11, this bunker was in use as a US Army command post. American field jackets can be seen at left, and a map case hangs from the gun barrel. NHHC 80-G-252574

Top: The kill zone of overlapping fire is evident in this photograph taken from one of the German pillboxes overlooking Omaha Beach. A German 88mm gun could easily engage any of the landing craft seen at water's edge, as well as many of the ships in the distance. NHHC 80-G-253256

Bottom: Looking down on the east end of Omaha Beach shows a line of destroyed LCVPs and LCPLs in the foreground, including a British *LCT-735* (closest to the camera at the shoreline). The old British battleship *Centurion* is seen in the distance, just to the left of center. *Centurion* was sunk to form part of the breakwater. NHHC 80-G-286425

A combat cameraman from the Ninth Air Force photographed this view of Omaha's Easy Green Beach from the hills near Saint-Laurent-sur-Mer, site of the first emergency airfield on French soil. Barrage balloons protect the assembled ships from low-flying German aircraft. NARA/US ARMY 51676AC

Facing page top: Looking down on the east end of the mulberry harbor protecting Omaha Beach shows the breakwater of sunken ships in the distance. On the beach, unloading operations continue with *LCT-149*, at left, and *LCT-195*, near the center of the image. Note seamen sitting with their gear in the center foreground and the Royal Navy vehicle at left. NHHC 80-G-286424

Facing page bottom: Men from the 834th Engineer Aviation Battalion look down on Omaha Beach. The unit is moving inland to carve out emergency landing strips and refueling and rearming airfields for the Ninth Air Force fighter-bombers that are supporting troops as they fight across France. NARA/US ARMY 76705AC

Pointe du Hoc had a commanding view of both Omaha Beach on the east side and Utah Beach on the west side. Allied air forces dropped more than 1,500 bombs on heavily fortified Pointe du Hoc. The bombing caused the Germans to remove the six 155mm cannon stationed there; however, its importance as an observation post was not lost on the Allies. They intended to take the prominent land feature with three companies of Rangers (2nd Ranger Battalion, Companies D, E, and F), who were to scale the 100-foot cliffs and secure the point.

Twelve landing craft and four DUKW trucks carrying 100-foot ladders were dispatched to assault the point. En route, two of the landing craft carrying supplies were sunk, one of the DUKWs went down, and a landing craft filled with Rangers was sunk, with only one survivor.

After landing and scaling the cliffs while taking high numbers of casualties, the Rangers secured the top of the point and then set off to find the guns. Five of the six 155mm cannon were found and destroyed by throwing thermite grenades down the barrels.

The Germans counterattacked on the night of June 6/7 and throughout the next day. It was not until June 8 that the Rangers were relieved and the area secured. NARA/US ARMY 52237AC

Facing page top: More akin to the lunar landscape than a beach in France, this view shows the devastation wrought by large-scale bombing and naval bombardment. An M29 Weasel is parked in a shell hole below grade to protect it from shell or bomb fragments, while barrage balloons have been assembled and inflated and are awaiting deployment. NARA/US ARMY 72624AC

Facing page bottom: German fortifications are seen in an early-morning aerial photo near St. Lô, France. Shot with an electronic flashbulb developed by the Air Technical Service Command and General Electric, the flash was effective at altitudes in excess of 500 feet. Three antiaircraft gun emplacements can be seen below the trenches. NARA/US ARMY 61566AC

REINFORCING THE BEACHHEAD

Facing page top: A fully loaded rhino ferry heads for the invasion beach under its own power. The shallow-draft barges could literally beach themselves at water's edge and discharge vehicles onto the sand. Here a mix of 2.5-ton trucks and trailers is moving forward. Notice the coxswain at the helm (in the center of the photo) surrounded by short railings, the 20mm antiaircraft gun, and the crew keeping a vigilant watch near the port rail. NHHC 80-G-59400

Facing page bottom: Looking to sea on June 10 shows a nearly empty rhino ferry with its loading ramp down, and a fully loaded rhino crossing in the background. *LCT-580*, beached at right, demonstrates the value of the shallow-draft rhinos, which enabled them to get farther up the beach to deliver men, vehicles, ammunition, and food supplies. Dozens of Liberty and Victory cargo ships obscure the horizon, and barrage balloons dot the sky while DUKW amphibious trucks can be seen shuttling supplies up the beach. NHHC 80-G-252647

Below: By June 12 the fighting had moved inland, away from the coast, a fact illustrated by the relaxed demeanor of the sailors on *LCI(L)-95*'s gangway. *LCI(L)-95* was part of LCI Flotilla 10, an all–Coast Guard flotilla. For Operation Neptune, the twenty-four Coast Guard LCI(L)s of Flotilla 10 were reinforced with the addition of twelve Navy-crewed LCI(L)s. Eighteen supported the invasion of Omaha Beach; the remaining eighteen were focused on Utah Beach. At Omaha Beach, four of the flotilla's LCI(L)s—*LCI(L)-85, -91, -92,* and *-93*—were destroyed and a number of others heavily damaged.

Coast Guard Lt. Robert M. Salmon, commanding officer of *LCI(L)-92*, was awarded the Silver Star for his actions on Omaha's Easy Green Beach. His citation reads: "For gallantry as commanding officer of a US LCI (L) while landing assault troops in Normandy, France, June 6, 1944. He pressed the landing of troops despite the mining of his vessel, a serious fire forward, and heavy enemy gunfire. He supervised the unloading of troops, directed the fire fighting despite the loss of proper equipment and exhibiting courage of a high degree remained with the ship until it was impossible to control the progress of the fire and it was necessary to abandon ship over the stern. After abandoning he directed a party searching for fire fighting equipment and subsequently fought the fire on another LCI (L) and assisted her commanding officer until she was abandoned." NHHC 80-G-252789

Left: The Landing Craft Support (Small) seen here on June 12 were used to support commandos, Army Rangers, and other small parties; in this case the boat is flying the pendant of a survey party. Although designated Landing Craft Support (Small), the boats were armed like a PT boat, with a pair of twin 0.50-caliber machine guns mounted in turrets on each side of the wheelhouse. One LCS(S) was lost on Omaha Beach on D-Day. NHHC 80-G-252685

Facing page top: An 80-foot-long Elco motor torpedo boat, more commonly known as a PT boat, escorts a troop ship across the English Channel. One PT boat was lost during Operation Neptune, coincidentally an Elco 80-foot boat, and that was *PT-505*. On the night of June 7, *PT-505* was chasing down what it thought was a submarine periscope in the waters off the Saint-Marcouf Islands, approximately 5.25 miles (8.4 km) off the coast of the Utah landing beach.

Just as the boat's skipper, Lt. William C. Godfrey (USN), was about to give the order to drop a depth charge on the suspected submarine, the PT boat struck an underwater mine. The boat's stern was lifted out of the water, and when it crashed back on the surface, both torpedo warheads broke loose and went over the side, a depth charge escaped its rack and went down, the engines were thrown from their mounts, and the boat was a mess. Two men were injured in the explosion.

PT-507 came to the boat's aid and took her in tow. Lieutenant Godfrey transferred the valuable radios and radar set to *PT-507* along with other equipment to lighten his boat. *PT-507* towed the crippled patrol boat to one of the Saint-Marcouf Islands, where the boat was beached and the hull patched. Once seaworthy again, *PT-505* was towed back across the Channel to Portland, England by PT-500; the craft finally arrived on June 11. NHHC 80-G-254261

Facing page bottom: Sailors watch as a jeep drives from inside *LST-282* into the bay of an LCT that will transfer it to the Omaha beachhead. The 20mm antiaircraft guns on both sides of the cargo well have additional ammunition magazines at the ready, while the LST's 40mm bow gun points skyward.

After supporting Operation Neptune, *LST-282* was transferred to Operation Dragoon, the invasion of southern France that began on August 15, 1944. Near the invasion beach off Boulouris, France, *LST-282* was struck by a German remote-control bomb, thought to be a Henschel HS-293. The explosion killed eleven men outright; thirty-nine more were unaccounted for. *LST-282* burned and was beached on Cape Dramont, France, and later scrapped in place. NHHC 80-G-253137

Top: *LST-21* unloads British Army trucks and an M4 Sherman tank on the afternoon of D-Day. The LST has docked to a rhino ferry that is being used as a pier. Later in June, *LST-21* carried a number of railcars across the English Channel. Engineers had laid a rail line to the beach, and the LST's bow ramp was fitted with the same. The railcars were connected and came off in-train. After Operation Overlord, *LST-21* supported Operation Dragoon in August 1944. NHHC/US COAST GUARD 26-G-2370

Bottom: Eight DUKWs make their way to the Normandy shore loaded with supplies. Cranes have placed nets loaded with everything from food to ammunition into the cargo compartment of the amphibious trucks. NARA

Top: A US Army Air Forces 23rd Photo Reconnaissance Squadron (PRS) portable darkroom comes ashore from an LST. The 23rd PRS had served in the Mediterranean Theater beginning in September 1943. The unit was stationed in Tunisia, on the Italian mainland, Sardinia, and Corsica before moving to Y-23, Valence Airfield, France, as Allied troops marched toward Germany. NARA/US ARMY 58710AC

Bottom: *LCT(5)-8* was laid down at the Manitowoc Ship Building Company in Manitowoc, Wisconsin, on July 15, 1942. Delivered to the US Navy on September 5 of that year, the landing craft was transferred to the Royal Navy through the Lend-Lease Program on September 28. The Royal Navy redesignated the craft HM *LCT-2008* and operated the tank landing craft in the Mediterranean Theater until early 1944, when it was reverse lend-leased to the US Navy. Redesignated as Landing Craft Tank (Armored) 2008 (*LCT[A]-2008*), this vessel was assigned to the LCT Gunfire Support Group. Sixteen LCT(A)s supported the landing at Omaha Beach, and eight delivered tanks to Utah Beach. Here, *LCT(A)-2008* is seen transporting troops from a ship to shore on June 7, 1944. NHHC 80-G-252719

On June 7, Royal Navy LCT (Mark VI)s *LCT-515* and *LCT-1048* offload men and equipment from the 834th Engineer Aviation Battalion at Omaha Beach. Note the CCKW truck with a Browning 0.50-caliber machine gun in an antiaircraft mount and the 834th Engineer Aviation Battalion bulldozer coming ashore. NARA/US ARMY 76708AC AND A-76710AC

Top: As territory near the coast fell and the threat of enemy shore fire was eliminated, minesweepers continued their work clearing the area of undersea explosives. Here a US Navy minesweeper (designated "YMS," for auxiliary motor minesweeper) detonates a pair of German undersea mines near the approaches to Cherbourg Harbor. NHHC 80-G-256041

Bottom: Aerial view of the Gold Beach area, where XXX Corps of the British Army, supported by troops from the Netherlands and Poland, came ashore to face the German Army's 352nd Infantry Division as well as the 716th Static Division. Within the boundaries of Gold Beach, the Germans had two large coastal batteries at Longues-sur-Mer (four 150mm guns) and Mont Fleury (four 122mm guns), which were priority targets of the Allied forces. Bombers had tried to silence these positions the night before, but it took soldiers on the ground to overwhelm the batteries. NARA/US ARMY 53519AC

SHIPS DAMAGED

Early during the invasion of Omaha Beach, *LCI(L)-85* struck a German underwater mine and was hit by more than twenty-five shells from coastal defense batteries. The landing craft infantry, crewed by US Coast Guard members, is making its way toward the attack transport *Samuel Chase* (APA-26), where she will offload her crew. NHHC 26-G-06-10-444

Facing page bottom: The Auk-class minesweeper *Tide* (AM-125) was assigned to Minesweeper Squadron A, tasked with clearing the sea in the vicinity of Utah Beach on D-Day. The following morning, as she was securing her minesweeping gear, *Tide* contacted a mine that broke the ship's back and killed her commanding officer, Lt. Cdr. Allard B. Heyward. *PT-509* (left) and minesweeper *Pheasant* (AM-61), at right, stood by to rescue survivors. The minesweeper *Swift* (AM-122) tried to tow *Tide* to the beach, but she broke in two and sank immediately. NHHC 80-G-651677

In the hours after the minesweeper *Tide* sank, the view off Omaha Beach on the morning of June 7 showed more stricken ships. *LCT(6)-714* from Flotilla 26 struck a mine and is seen with her bow pointing skyward as another crippled LCI, most likely from Flotilla 10, sits on the beach. NHHC 80-G-252437

At 4:00 on the morning of June 10, Liberty Ship *Charles Morgan* was struck by a 500-pound (226.7-kg) bomb, which impacted the number-five cargo hatch, blowing off the cover and rupturing the main deck. One member of the ship's crew and seven members of her gun crew were killed in the attack. Hull plating on the ship's port side was opened to the sea from the number-four hold aft to the auxiliary steering engine room. Moored in 33 feet of water, *Charles Morgan*'s stern settled to the bottom. Attempts were made to salvage the ship, but the damage was too extensive. *LCT-474* and the fleet tug *Kiowa* (ATF-72) are seen alongside, rendering aid. NHHC 80-G-252657 AND 80-G-252655

EMERGENCY INVASION HARBORS

This phoenix caisson, built at southern England's Portsmouth Dockyard, is positioned for its tow across the Channel, where it will help form a breakwater for the mulberry artificial harbors. More than 210 of the phoenix caissons were built in different sizes, the largest 200 feet long, 60 feet tall, with an overall weight of 6,000 tons. Two mulberries were planned—one off Omaha Beach (known as Mulberry A) and the other, Mulberry B, known as "Port Winston," to supply the British, Canadian, and Free French troops at Gold Beach near Arromanches-les-Bains, France. Mulberry A was wrecked in a storm on June 19, while Mulberry B/Port Winston was in service for nearly 10 months, bringing more than 4 million tons of supplies, 2.5 million men, and more than 500,000 vehicles ashore. NHHC 80-G-251981

US Army oceangoing tug *ST-759* maneuvers an unidentified Liberty ship into position to be sunk to form a gooseberry breakwater. Gooseberry breakwaters were constructed at Utah, Omaha, Gold, Juno, and Sword Beaches, numbered 1 to 5, respectively. Vessels identifiable in the background are *LCI(L)-86* (center), British *LCT-930* (right), and British *LCT-763* (extreme right). NHHC 80-G-286402

Top: Work to clear the beaches of German obstacles and mines got underway as soon as the fighting moved out of range. This photograph of the Omaha Beach area was taken on June 11 and shows a pile of "Czech hedgehog" anti-invasion steel obstacles. The hedgehogs take their name from their original location along the German–Czechoslovak border and were first seen in 1935–1936. The line of ships on the horizon is a gooseberry breakwater consisting of fifty-five ships purposely sunk to provide a breakwater protecting Omaha Beach. NHHC 80-G-252753

Bottom: A pontoon causeway sits on Omaha Beach at low tide on June 12. The line of ships in the distance forms part of the gooseberry breakwater. The tidal range of the Normandy beaches during the war was 22 feet. NHHC 80-G-252793

Top: Omaha Beach fortifications with antitank barriers and barbed wire seen from German positions behind barbed-wire defenses. Note the depth of the anti-invasion defenses at low tide. The invasion fleet rides at anchor in the background. BUNDESARCHIV BILD 101I-493-3363-13

Bottom: A wide variety of cargo and obsolete military ships were sunk to form the gooseberry breakwaters to protect the invasion beaches. Photographed from a low-flying Ninth Air Force Martin B-26 Marauder, the scene shows nine Liberty ships in position as a protecting screen for vessels unloading on the beach. Additional block ships (code-named "corncobs") would be brought in to expand the breakwater in the coming days. NARA/USAAF 54684AC

Nearly every type of vessel supporting the invasion can be seen in this photo of the gooseberry breakwater off Omaha Beach. Everything from Liberty cargo ships to rhino ferries plies the waters moving supplies to the beachhead. At this point, fifteen Liberty ships have been sunk to form the gooseberry breakwater, with more ships to come. NARA/USAAF 54577AC

CASUALTIES, RESCUES, EVACUATIONS

Left: Midday on D-Day, Coast Guardsmen rescue survivors from the sea. To the right, behind the rescuers, appears to be a minesweeper. NHHC/US COAST GUARD 26-G-2375

Below left and right: An LCM (landing craft mechanized) brings wounded to a transport ship for medical attention. Most appear to be ambulatory; however, transferring the wounded from sea level up to the ship's main deck often required using cranes. NHHC/US COAST GUARD 26-G-2386

Right: The sinking Coast Guard–manned USS *LCI(L)-85* comes alongside *Samuel Chase* (APA-26) to transfer her survivors after she struck a mine and was hit by German shells off Omaha Beach on D-Day. A wartime censor has obscured the face of the soldier lying on the stretcher; a deceased soldier to the right has his head and face covered with a jacket. NHHC/US COAST GUARD 26-G-2344

Top: A life cut short: An American soldier lies where he fell during the initial assault on Omaha Beach. Based upon his location far from the seawall, he may have drowned while exiting his landing craft. An M1 Garand and an M1903 rifle lie near his feet. Note how the Germans used tree trunks as well as Czech hedgehogs as anti-invasion obstacles. NHHC/US COAST GUARD 26-G-2397

Bottom: The cost of war captured on film on Omaha Beach, D-Day, June 6, 1944. These men were members of the 3rd Battalion, 16th Infantry Regiment, 1st Infantry Division. Some of the men have been covered by life belts, while a box shields the face of another dead soldier. NHHC/SIGNAL CORPS SC 189924

Right: Wounded
soldiers from the
3rd Battalion, 16th
Infantry Regiment, 1st
Infantry Division, await
evacuation off the
beach to troop ships
and more intensive
medical care after they
drove the Germans from
Omaha Beach. NHHC/
SIGNAL CORPS SC 189910

Captured German soldiers march out on June 12 to waiting ships that will take them to captivity. Their
capture at Normandy essentially guaranteed these men would survive the war. Prisoner of war camps
in England, Canada, and the United States warehoused captured German soldiers for the duration of
the war. The Allies took 47,000 prisoners in June and 36,000 in July, with 150,000 captured in August
1944. NHHC 80-G-252828

CHAPTER THREE

Securing a Foothold on the Continent

The end of the day on June 6 saw the Allies firmly ashore, but in a tenuous position. Assault troops from the beaches were holding ground up to 5 and 6 miles inland. To make the advance more difficult, the Germans had flooded the low-lying areas behind the beaches, turning many of the fields into swamps.

The first link between American seaborne forces and airborne infantry took place at Pouppeville, about 1 mile in from the coast. The 3rd Battalion, 501st Parachute Infantry Regiment, 101st Airborne Division, was dropped off course and had to regroup. Only able to locate forty of the regiment's men, Lt. Col. Julian J. Ewell pressed ahead to take the village of Pouppeville, which sat across one of the roads, known as Exit 1, leading across the flooded fields and inland. A force of little more than sixty men from the 1058th Grenadier Regiment from the German 91st Infantry Division held the town and put up fierce resistance. The Grenadiers killed eighteen Americans and lost twenty-five of their own, with another thirty-eight Grenadiers surrendering around noon. The 2nd Battalion, 8th Infantry Regiment, 4th Infantry Division, which had come ashore at Utah Beach, joined the 501st at Pouppeville to make the first seaborne/airborne troop connection of D-Day.

The 8th Infantry Regiment and other units of the 4th Infantry Division moved out to relieve the 82nd Airborne at Sainte-Mère-Église while the 2nd Ranger Battalion continued to hold Pointe du Hoc. Overnight, the 2nd Rangers fought a fierce battle with the German 914th Grenadier Regiment. The 914th nearly forced the Rangers back into the sea, reducing the ground the

Americans held to a section of the cliffs only 200 yards wide. Twenty-three men from the 5th Ranger Battalion were able to join the 2nd Rangers during the night to help hold off repeated German counterattacks. On June 7, the Rangers were supplied from the sea by a pair of landing craft that brought food, water, and ammunition, but no fresh troops. It took another full day of fighting before men from the 2nd and 5th Rangers, the 1st Battalion, 116th Infantry Regiment, and the 743rd Tank Battalion were able to break the stalemate and relieve the Rangers. More than 125 Rangers were lost assaulting and holding Pointe du Hoc.

To the east of Omaha and Utah Beaches, the British and Canadians were having just as hard a time with the Atlantic Wall's defenses. At Gold Beach, the British met very light resistance and were able to move inland fairly fast. Free French and British Commandos moved off Sword Beach quickly and were able to take Hermanville and Ouistreham before noon. However, the amount of Allied troops and vehicles landing in subsequent waves choked the narrow French country roads and brought the advance to a halt, completely destroying the plan to take the town of Caen by midnight. Shortly thereafter, the British Suffolk Regiment ran into the German strongpoint known as WN17 (or to the British as the Hillman Fortress) near Ouistreham, home to the 736th Grenadier Regiment. It took until 8:00 on the night of June 6 to rout the Germans from the complex.

ADVANCE BASES

While land troops were slowly advancing, capturing ground from the Germans, Allied engineer battalions were also ashore and busy scraping French soil. They were turning farm fields into airfields to provide the infrastructure needed to maintain air superiority to protect Allied troops. The Americans sent two airborne aviation engineering battalions and sixteen engineer (aviation) battalions, while the British landed five airfield construction groups and four airfield construction wings. By the time all these units were ashore, they counted nearly 64,000 men—all dedicated to building infrastructure for Allied aircraft.

Engineers built five different types of airfields, each to meet a different need of the Allied air forces. First to be carved out of the countryside were a series of emergency landing strips: scraped earth, level, and a minimum of 1,800 feet long—just enough to give a pilot in a damaged aircraft a safe haven rather than tempting fate by trying to cross the English Channel in a marginally airworthy plane.

The next level of airfield was built to increase the amount of air cover provided to ground troops. Rather than having a fighter/bomber fly from its base in England, across the Channel, and then to the target—a minimum of thirty minutes flying time each way—refueling and rearming strips were built to service aircraft and get them back into the action as soon as possible. Fighters would begin their day in England, attack targets in France, refuel and rearm at a local strip, and continue flying sorties until it was time to retire across the Channel for the night. The third type advance landing grounds, had dispersal areas large enough to accommodate two squadrons for extended periods, which could then be rotated out with fresh squadrons. These airfields were larger, more permanent facilities, able to accommodate fifty-four aircraft, and provided all the support that would be found on bases back in England. Hard-surface, all-weather airfields took the longest to construct, as they were much larger facilities with paved runways.

Operation Overlord contained an aggressive schedule for the construction of airfields in the captured areas, and two were open for business on D-Day Plus One (June 7). As the airfields came online, each was given an identifier denoting which service was the primary tenant; American airfields were assigned an "A" followed by a number; British airfields were given a "B" and a number. Emergency Landing Strip 1 at Pouppeville, behind Utah Beach; B-1 at Asnelles-sur-Mer, inland from Gold Beach; and A-21C at Saint-Laurent-sur-Mer were open for business by the end of June 7—the first of more than sixty constructed between D-Day and August 31.

A-21C was built by the IX Engineer Command's 834th Engineer (Aviation) Battalion on top of the bluffs overlooking Omaha Beach between Les Moulins to the west and Saint-Laurent-sur-Mer to the east. The strip was 3,400 feet long and was prepared in sixteen hours. The strip's proximity to the invasion beaches enabled the battalion's heavy construction and earth-moving equipment to go into action quickly. This airfield was immediately used by Troop Carrier Command C-47s to evacuate wounded back to hospitals in England within a matter of hours of a soldier's being injured.

CAEN AND THE BIG PRIZE: THE PORT OF CHERBOURG

On June 12, the US First Army took the town of Carentan, the key to strangling German troops on the Cotentin Peninsula, which in turn leads to the port of Cherbourg. Following a brutal battle against superior Allied forces, Cherbourg and most of the surrounding areas surrendered on June 29. German resistance

was determined, as repeated attempts to take Caen failed, and the city was reduced to rubble through aerial bombardment. When the buildings fell from exploding bombs, the rubble choked the streets, impeding Allied tanks while creating vast numbers of defensive positions for the Germans. After continued heavy fighting, the city was finally liberated on July 9. Simultaneously to the attempts to take Caen, Allied troops attacked St. Lô on July 3. The Germans resisted for more than two weeks before the Allies were able to dislodge the defenders on July 18.

Gen. Omar Bradley's Operation Cobra, July 25–31, employing strategic bombers to pulverize German armor, essentially ended the Normandy Campaign and enabled the Allies to break out and begin the march across France. On August 1, the US Third Army under the command of Gen. George S. Patton was added to the battle. Patton's troops marched into Le Mans on August 8, and soon German Army Group B, the Seventh Army, and the Fifth Panzer Army were surrounded between the cities of Falaise (27 miles/44 km south of Caen) and Chambois. Known as the Battle of the Falaise Gap, the Allies nearly annihilated Army Group B, breaking the back of German resistance in the region.

The loss of an estimated forty German divisions in Normandy between June 6 and August 15 enabled the Allies to drive across France and liberate Paris on August 25. There was more bloody, costly fighting ahead, but the Allies had opened a second front. The end for Nazi Germany was now only nine months in the future.

Below: US Army Rangers rest atop the cliffs at Pointe du Hoc on the afternoon of June 8. The cliffs, which towered more than 100 feet above sea level, divided the Utah and Omaha landing beaches. On top of Pointe du Hoc were six 155mm guns, four in concrete casemates. The US Ninth Air Force bombed the area in April, and the Germans subsequently removed the guns. However, Allied planners wanted to prevent the Germans from using Pointe du Hoc as an observation post to direct fire down onto the invasion beaches. The 2nd Ranger Battalion was put ashore from British landing craft while the battleship USS *Texas* (BB-35), destroyer USS *Satterlee* (DD-626), and Royal Navy Hunt-Class destroyer HMS *Talybont* bombarded the top of the cliffs. The Rangers took the point and subsequently found five of the six 155mm guns, which they destroyed. It was not until June 8 that the Rangers were relieved; in the final tally, 135 of the 225 men who assaulted the cliffs were killed. NARA 80-G-45721

Above: One of the four 152mm coastal defense guns at the Longues-sur-Mer battery is seen as engineers dismantle its gun tube. The battery was sited between the American Omaha Beach and the British Gold Beach objectives.

Hours before the invasion landings, RAF Bomber Command aircraft launched a massive raid against the coastal batteries at Fontenay, Houlgate, La Pernelle, Longues-sur-Mer, Maisy, Merville, Mont Fleury, and Pointe du Hoc. Exactly 1,012 aircraft were dispatched on the raid, with 946 making the drops. More than 5,000 tons of bombs were dropped, of which 1,500 tons were aimed at the Longues-sur-Mer battery complex. Unfortunately, the majority of the bombs fell into the nearby town.

The US Navy battleship *Arkansas* (BB-33), the French cruiser *Georges Leygues*, and the Royal Navy cruisers *Ajax* and *Argonaut* all shelled the battery, with *Ajax* and *Argonaut* scoring direct hits, disabling three of the four guns. The single remaining gun continued to fire throughout the day, but on June 7 the battery's crew of 184 men surrendered to the British Army's 231st Infantry Brigade. NARA/ USAAF 72627AC

Facing page bottom: Street scene in Villers-Bocage showing the aftermath of strafing by RAF Typhoons and USAAF Thunderbolts. German tracked vehicles, guns, and trucks have been devastated by cannon shells and 0.50-caliber bullets raining down from Allied fighters. BUNDESARCHIV BILD 101-738-0267-21A

EVACUATING THE WOUNDED

The Overlord plan called for the immediate construction of three emergency landing strips by the end of D-Day—a tall order considering the German opposition faced by Allied troops. Once available, C-47s of the Ninth Air Force Air Evacuation Unit began ferrying wounded soldiers, sailors, airmen, and German prisoners back to England and its rear-area hospitals. Note the barrage balloon and ships seen in the distance over the C-47's number-one engine. Round circles in the C-47's windows are gun ports, enabling soldiers on board to fire their weapons without fully opening the windows. NARA/USAAF 51923AC AND 51858AC

RESUPPLYING THE FRONT

S/Sgt. George Blinkinsop of Clinton, Iowa, with clipboard, checks off a DUKW load of ammunition destined for Ninth Air Force fighters at a nearby advance landing field. The DUKW is a 6-wheel, 2.5-ton amphibious truck with a payload of 5,000 pounds (2,300 kg) or 24 troops. The acronym stood for D (designed in 1942), U (utility), K (all-wheel drive), and W (dual-tandem rear axles). DUKWs could operate in fairly rough seas, and one was even driven/sailed across the English Channel. NARA/USAAF 121821AC

The Ninth Air Force made extensive use of parapacks to resupply troops once on the continent.
NARA/USAAF

A IX Troop Carrier Command C-47 delivers an Army jeep to a forward airfield. Note the spade and HQ markings on the jeep's bumper. NARA/USAAF 52033AC

Auxiliary fuel tanks extend an aircraft's range when escorting bombers or provide longer loiter times for fighter-bombers attacking road and rail traffic, convoys, bridges, and troop concentrations. Once a pilot has drained the fuel from the tanks, they are released, or dropped, to reduce aerodynamic drag on the aircraft. The only problem with dropping the tanks is that they are lost and thus not reusable. Here two semitruck loads of auxiliary fuel tanks have been brought ashore from a IX Air Service Command depot and are making their way to an advance airfield on the continent to aid in the air war against Germany.

NARA/USAAF 55611AC

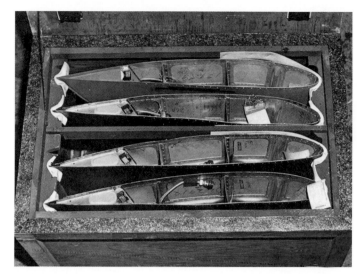

The Army Air Forces developed "compaks" to supply forward-deployed aircraft maintainers. Each compak was limited to 200 pounds; here four wing tips are shown. The removal of one wing tip does not impact the others, and once empty, the compaks could be returned to depots in England to be refilled. NARA/USAAF 81261AC

ADVANCE BASES

Aerial view of the airfield at Saint-Pierre-du-Mont (A-1) showing how close the field was to the coast and the flotilla of supply ships off the landing beaches. This photo was shot after the battle had moved inland, as P-38 Lightnings and P-47 Thunderbolts can be seen disbursed around the field. Pointe du Hoc is visible at the upper left side of the photo. NARA/USAAF 77061AC

Above: The first Lockheed P-38 Lightning to land on the continent was P-38J 42-68071, seen touching down at Saint-Pierre-du-Mont (A-1) on June 10. Once the ground was taken after the invasion, this area was cleared for use as a crash strip to give damaged aircraft a place to land if they could not make it back across the English Channel to safety. Although graded earth in this photo, the field was later paved. The Piper L-4 to the right was used in the scout and artillery spotter role. NARA/SIGNAL CORPS 190118-S

Below: As the battle moved inland, this C-47 from the 434th Troop Carrier Group, 72nd Troop Carrier Squadron, unloads supplies at a captured German airfield. This aircraft (fuselage code 6U-A) was factory-fresh, having been delivered to the Army Air Forces on April 27, 1944, and assigned to the Ninth Air Force on May 28, 1944. Its career was short-lived, however as 43-15663 was shot down on September 18, 1944, near Boxtel, Noord-Brabant, the Netherlands, while towing a glider during Operation Market Garden. NARA/USAAF 53615AC

Top: A P-47 departs Saint-Pierre-du-Mont (A-1), shortly after the strip opened for business. Damaged fighters and fighter-bombers could land at the crash strip, built by the 834th Engineer Aviation Battalion, without having to risk a flight across the English Channel. The efforts of the engineer battalions saved the lives of many aircrewmen in the days following the invasion. Fighters could also land at A-1 for fuel and ammunition to maintain longer patrols over enemy territory. NARA/USAAF 51862AC

Bottom: Lockheed F-5B, the photo reconnaissance version of the P-38, is seen being serviced in England after overflying the landing beaches in France. This F-5B was flown by Lt. Col. C. A. Shoop, commander of the 7th Photographic Reconnaissance Group, Eighth Air Force, which was based at USAAF Station 234, RAF Mount Farm. Shoop and his group photographed the battle at Omaha Beach and provided photos to advise General Eisenhower of the invasion's progress. Shoop ended his military career as a major general in the California Air National Guard. NARA/USAAF 54574AC

Top: P-47D-6-RE 42-74629, *Snuffy/Times A Wastin'*, at Saint-Pierre-du-Mont (A-1) during the opening days of the campaign. *Snuffy/Times A Wastin'* was attached to the 48th Fighter Group, 492nd Fighter Squadron (fuselage code F4), based at USAAF Station 347/RAF Ibsley. On June 18, the 48th Fighter Group moved across the channel to Deux Jumeaux Airfield (A-4), France. The group concentrated on dive-bombing bridges, roads, and rail lines; by the time the campaign was over, the group had flown almost 2,000 sorties and dropped 500 tons of bombs. NARA/USAAF 76651AC

Bottom: P-47D-22-RE 42-25683, *Miss Lace*, of the 48th Fighter Group, 492nd Fighter Squadron (fuselage code F4-C), seen at Deux Jumeaux (A-4) being serviced in preparation for another mission. Note the ground crew taking a break on a drop tank, seen under the wing near the main landing gear. NARA/USAAF A17545

Top: P-47s of the 371st Fighter Group, 404th Fighter Squadron, in line for servicing after a mission. Aircraft of the 404th Fighter Squadron wore the fuselage code 9Q. The second aircraft from the right is P-47D-15-RE 42-76172 (fuselage code 9Q-N), flown by 2nd Lt. John E. Bailey. During the afternoon of July 30, 1944, Bailey was flying an armed reconnaissance mission in the vicinity of Pont-Bellanger when his aircraft was singled out by flak batteries. Flight leader Maj. Rodney E. Gunther saw Bailey's cockpit on fire, then watched as the aircraft fell off to the right and crashed on its back, exploding. NARA/USAAF

Bottom: P-47D-28-RE 44-20201 (fuselage code 9Q-J) is seen taxiing out for a dive-bombing mission with 500-pound bombs under each wing and antipersonnel cluster bomblets on the center hardpoint.

This aircraft was later written off on April 10, 1945, when it was damaged beyond repair in a ground loop on landing at Eschborn (Y-74), on the outskirts of Frankfurt, Germany. Pilot Lt. Lyman L. Lyons had previously had to put P-47D-28-RE 44-19782 down in a field in bad weather on February 6, 1945, near Chaumont, France. NARA/USAAF 56316-A

Facing page top: Wearing invasion stripes, P-47D-27-RE 42-27376 (fuselage code 9Q-R) of the 371st Fighter Group, 404th Fighter Squadron, taxies out for a dive-bombing mission with a 500-pound bomb on the centerline hardpoint (between the main landing gear). On D-Day, the 404th Fighter Squadron escorted gliders to Sainte-Mère-Église, then dive-bombed and strafed the beaches. Months later, during the drive across France, this aircraft was damaged by flak and crash-landed near Etzling on the French side of the German border near Saarbrücken. NARA/USAAF

Facing page bottom: Hectic scene at Saint-Pierre-du-Mont (A-1) as Thunderbolts from various squadrons land to refuel and rearm as they strafe and dive-bomb German troops and emplacements in the Normandy area. At left is Lt. Herbert H. Stachler's P-47D-22-RE 42-26278 (fuselage code A8-Y), *Lil Herbie*, from the 366th Fighter Group, 391st Fighter Squadron, which was a tenant unit at A-1. Stachler flew two missions on D-Day in *Lil Herbie*. He survived the war and was separated at the rank of captain. P-47D *Lil Herbie* was later shot down by an Fw 190 on December 24, 1944, over the Ahrweiler district south of Bonn, Germany, killing pilot 2nd Lt. John K. Jones Jr.

In the distant center of the photo is a Thunderbolt (fuselage code CH) from the 358th Fighter Group's 365th Fighter Squadron, which, at the time of this photo, was based at USAAF Station 411, RAF High Halden, in Kent, England. At right is a 405th Fighter Group, 509th Fighter Squadron, Thunderbolt (wearing fuselage code G9) that was based at USAAF Station 416, RAF Christchurch, in Dorset, England. NARA/USAAF

Below: The 50th Fighter Group moved to Carentan (A-10), about 9 miles (15 km) south of Utah Beach, on June 25. P-47D-22-RE 42-25904 (fuselage code 2N-U), *Lethal Liz II*, the mount of 2nd Lt. Arthur Davis, and another 313th Fighter Squadron Thunderbolt wait for the next mission while cows graze in their midst. A number of damaged aircraft line the perimeter of the airfield, with a P-51 Mustang behind the two 313th Fighter Squadron aircraft; an RAF Supermarine Spitfire operated by US Navy Cruiser Scouting Squadron Seven (VCS-7) that suffered a belly landing and a P-47 with a collapsed right main gear can be seen in the distance. Pilots from VCS-7 swapped their usual slow-moving SOC floatplanes for Spitfires to direct naval bombardment against shore targets behind enemy lines. NARA/USAAF 52657AC

A French narrow-gauge railway has been put back into service by members of the 354th Fighter Group. The ore cars carry pilots out to their disbursed aircraft and are also used to carry tools, ammunition, and other service items around the airstrip. The P-51B in the background (wearing fuselage code AJ-S) belongs to the 354th Fighter Group, 356th Fighter Squadron, and is seen at Circqueville (A-2). NARA/ USAAF 53844AC

AIR COMBAT

Deception played a large role during Operation Overlord, on both sides. The Allies had Operation Fortitude, which falsely threatened an invasion force sailing from Scotland to invade Norway, as well as Operation Quicksilver, a cross-Channel landing at Calais. To sell Operation Quicksilver, Lt. Gen. George S. Patton was put in charge of the fictional First US Army Group. Wood-and-fabric tanks and trucks were constructed all over the south of England to give German aerial reconnaissance the impression of a large troop buildup.

Simultaneously, the Germans were employing the same techniques of deception to mislead the Allies as to their strength. Once on French soil, and as Allied troops began capturing Luftwaffe airfields, the extent of the Germans' use of decoys became evident. Here stacks of former Luftwaffe "aircraft," complete down to squadron markings on the fuselages, are prepared for the bonfire. NARA/USAAF 52870

Facing page bottom: The picturesque stone railroad bridge that crosses the Loire River at the town of Orléans lost ten of its fourteen spans during a June 15 bombing raid. The only human casualty was a sentry patrolling the bridge at the time of the attack. Dropping the bridges prevented the Germans from reinforcing their frontline troops and enabled the Allies to contain the enemy. NARA/USAAF K2786

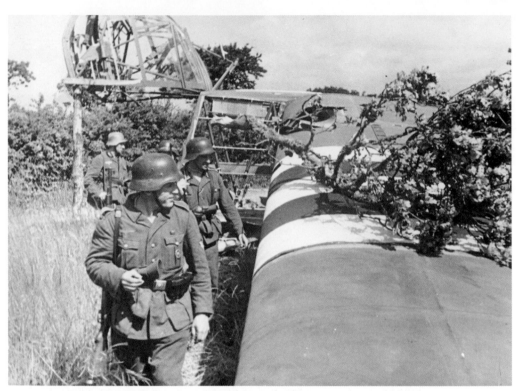

Above: A German patrol inspects a Waco CG-4A glider that was slated to land in Drop Zone W as part of Mission Elmira. The glider carried members and equipment of the 82nd Airborne Division. The original caption, in German, implies that the pilot and copilot were killed in the landing and the soldiers inside were taken prisoner. Based on the amount of missing fabric from the nose and fuselage, and the lack of fire, it appears this glider was heavily souvenired by German soldiers. BUNDESARCHIV BILD 146-2004-0176

Facing page: Ninth Air Force Douglas A-20G-30-DO 43-9502, from the 410th Bomb Group, 644th Bomb Squadron (fuselage code 5D), took off from USAAF Station 154, RAF Gosfield on August 4 to bomb the double roadway bridge across the Seine River at Rouen, France. The target was obscured by clouds, which required the bomber formation to make a second run at the target. By this time German flak gunners had their range, and a photographer in another A-20 caught the destruction of 43-9502. Leaving the target area, the Havoc's bomb bay doors are open as the flak bursts around the bomber. Moments later the bomb bay doors have been closed as a direct flak hit severs the Havoc's empennage. The vertical fin can be seen above the aircraft's left engine as the bomber comes apart. Pilot 1st Lt. Thomas G. Walsh perished when the tailless bomber crashed near Grand-Couronne, south of Rouen. Both gunners, S/Sgt. Fred Herman and Sgt. Karl W. Haeuser, were taken prisoner. NARA/USAAF 53119AC

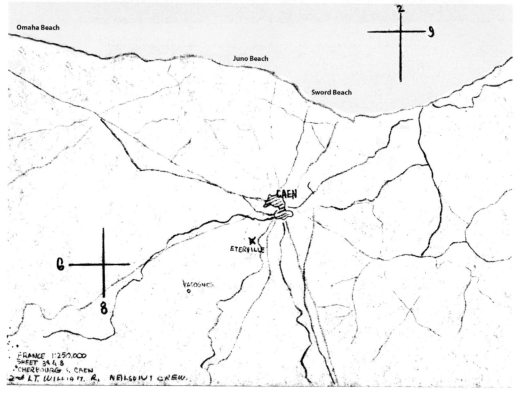

Facing page: Flying at 11,500 feet en route to bomb road targets on June 13, B-26C 42-107682, *Hannibal Hoops*, from the 587th Bomb Squadron (fuselage code 5W), 394th Bomb Group, was flying in the formation's second box, low flight, in the number-three position. Approximately thirty seconds before the bombs were to be dropped on a road junction in the Caen area, flak tore off the port engine and another shell exploded in the cockpit, igniting the forward fuselage. The bomber came down between Étavaux and Eterville, less than 4.5 miles (7 km) from Caen's town square (see map bottom page 164).

    The crew consisted of 2nd Lt. William R. Nielsen, pilot; 2nd Lt. Donald B. Damer, copilot; Sgt. Jack R. King, bombardier; S/Sgt. Adam Toth, engineer-gunner; Sgt. Elmer Fellhauer, radio operator/gunner; and S/Sgt. Gervaise F. Jarmer, tail gunner. Nielsen, Damer, and King in the front of the Marauder perished; Fellhauer, Jarmer, and Toth, stationed in the rear of the bomber, were able to bail out. All three became POWs, with Toth later escaping from a POW work farm and evading recapture. BUNDESARCHIV BILD 101I-299-1819-21A; MAP FROM MACR 6048

Lt. Col. Marshall Cloke (second from right) was the squadron commander of the 354th Fighter Group's 380th Fighter Squadron. Cloke is seen reviewing mission details with his flight leaders before heading to attack German supply and communications targets. Left to right: Capt. Clayton Kelly Gross (Spokane, Washington), Maj. Gilbert Talbot (Clackamas, Oregon), Cloke (Albuquerque, New Mexico), and Capt. Lewis W. Powers (Compton, California). Gross had five kills to his credit when this photo was taken in late June 1944. He flew 105 missions during two tours with the 355th Fighter Squadron, while Talbot had downed three at this point. Talbot finished the war with five kills, scoring his fourth and fifth victories in March and April 1945 over Bf 109s. NARA/USAAF 56037AC

Top: Maj. Gordon J. Burris (left) interviews Col. George R. Bickell (right) after the first Mustang mission of D-Day. Bickell was a flight commander with the 18th Pursuit Group stationed at Hickam Field, Territory of Hawaii, from 1940 through the Japanese attack on Pearl Harbor and America's entry into the war to 1942. He became commanding officer of the 354th Fighter Group on April 17, 1944, and served in that capacity until February 28, 1945. He was credited with 3.5 aerial victories. Behind Bickell and to the right is ace Capt. Clayton Kelly Gross, who would shoot down a German Me 262 jet fighter on April 14, 1945, for his sixth victory. NARA/USAAF 53433AC

Bottom: First Lt. John J. Donnelan stands next to his Piper L-4H-Pl 43-29676. In civilian use, the L-4 is the J-3 Cub, and numerous examples were pressed into service when the war broke out. The tandem, two-seat L-4 is powered by a 75-horsepower Continental A75-9 flat-four-cylinder engine. These aircraft were perfect artillery-spotter planes and were also used extensively for liaison work, as they could take off and land in short distances from unimproved airstrips. NARA/USAAF 53827AC

Top: A field of Piper L-4s, with 43-30338 in the foreground. The aircraft seen here have recently been removed from shipping crates, assembled, and are ready for test flights. These aircraft had fixed-pitch propellers and were manually started by ground crew hand-spinning the prop. L-4s and their companion Stinson L-5s were known as "The Grasshopper Fleet" due to their small size and green color. NARA/USAAF 53739

Bottom: Capt. Randall W. Hendricks discusses future targets with a US Army cavalry officer alongside P-47D-21-RA 43-25570, *Kwit-Cher-Bitchin* (fuselage code D3-H). Note the servicing cart behind the Thunderbolt stacked with 5-gallon jerry cans of aviation gasoline. This photo was taken at the 368th Fighter Group, 397th Fighter Squadron's first home on the continent at Cardonville (A-3). On June 12, Hendricks shot down four Fw 190s and damaged a fifth 5 miles north of Lisieux (about 25 miles/40 km east of Caen). Ten days later, on June 22, Hendricks shot down a Bf 109 and damaged another, earning him the title of "ace." NARA/USAAF 80087A

Above: P-47 42-76127, *Turnip Termite*, of the 365th Fighter Group, 387th Fighter Squadron, was the personal mount of Capt. Arlo Henry. Returning from a mission, Henry ran out of fuel and tried to land at A-21C at Saint-Laurent-sur-Mer. Without enough altitude to glide to the airfield, he belly-landed *Turnip Termite* into a minefield instead. The aircraft was recovered and is seen upon arrival at A-21C, where it was stripped and subsequently scrapped. NARA/USAAF

Facing page top: The dangers of strafing trains are evident on the battered leading edge of Lt. Howard A. Spaulding's 361st Fighter Group, 375th Fighter Squadron, P-51 Mustang. Flying low to score hits on a German train near Chartres, France, he descended too low and struck a tree. Able to maintain flight after impacting the tree, Spaulding managed to return to base. The wing's missing leading edge looks as though it once held an additional 0.50-caliber machine gun. NARA/USAAF 51977

Facing page bottom: Hit by flak, his plane's hydraulics shot out, and seriously wounded, pilot Lt. Jacob C. Blazicek brought his Thunderbolt in for an emergency landing at Cardonville (A-3) on June 17. Blazicek was knocked unconscious when the aircraft nosed-over and came to an abrupt stop. The aircraft, P-47D-20-RE 42-76436 (fuselage code CP-D) from the 358th Fighter Group, 367th Fighter Squadron, was salvaged for parts. Lieutenant Blazicek was hospitalized, eventually recovering from his wounds. Note the heavy flak damage to the port wing, flap, and aileron.

The 816th Engineer Aviation Battalion began work on the advance landing ground at Cardonville on June 7, about twenty-four hours after the invasion began. The airstrip was ready to receive aircraft by June 10, and four days later the P-47 Thunderbolts of the 368th Fighter Group began using A-3 as a forward rearming and refueling base. On June 19, the group moved from RAF Station 485, Greenham Common, England, to A-3, becoming the first fighter group stationed and operational on the European continent. NARA/USAAF 80022AC

French pilots of the "Escadrille Lafayette" were equipped with Republic P-47 Thunderbolts to help liberate their home country. The insignia of the Lafayette Escadrille, America's iconic volunteer squadron that fought alongside the French during World War I before the United States officially entered the conflict, was selected to honor the bravery of the prior conflict's pilots and the relationship between the two nations. From left, Lieutenants Pierre Chanoine, Jean Honnorat (in cockpit), Henri Ducru, Jacques Maleville, and Jean Marillonnet study a map before strafing and dive-bombing enemy fortifications in the path of Allied armies. NARA/USAAF 56219AC

S/Sgt. Harold Staugler, crew chief, of Fort Recovery, Ohio, works on the landing gear oleo of North American P-51B-15-NA 42-106897, *Rigor Mortis III* (fuselage code FT-V). The aircraft is seen at Cricqueville Airfield (A-2) behind the invasion beaches. *Rigor Mortis III* was the personal aircraft of 1st Lt. Edward R. Regis from the 354th Fighter Group, 353rd Fighter Squadron. Regis was credited with three aerial victories, two of which have been recorded on the fuselage under the windscreen. Note how crudely the invasion stripes were applied, especially on the lowered flaps. NARA/USAAF 53860

Soldiers stand by the wing of P-51D-5-NA 44-13309, *Fools Paradise IV*, as other 363rd Fighter Group Mustangs return to Azeville Airfield (A-7). *Fools Paradise IV* (fuselage code A9-A) was the personal mount of Maj. Evan McCall. This Mustang flew with the Ninth Air Force, 363rd Fighter Group, 380th Fighter Squadron, and on D-Day the group flew cover for troop transports and gliders as they made their way across the Channel to the drop and landing zones. NARA/USAAF 52356AC

A jeep from the 363rd Fighter Group, 380th Fighter Squadron, wears pinup art on its canvas door cover, used to keep mud from splashing its occupants. The art is Alberto Vargas's *Esquire* magazine pinup "Sleepy-Time Gal." This pinup appeared on aircraft ranging from B-17 and B-24 bombers to a US Navy F4F Wildcat fighter. NARA/USAAF

Cpl. Carl D. Knox (left) of Syracuse, New York, and Cpl. Alfred Van Drake of Newark, New York, install an aerial camera into an F-6C (photo reconnaissance version of the P-51B). The F-6C could be fitted with two K24 cameras (or one K17 and one K22 camera). Knox is holding a K22 camera, which used a 9 × 9-inch canister of roll film with 200 exposures and was capable of vertical or oblique photography. Note the application of invasion stripes to this aircraft. NARA/USAAF 54734AC

Above: Early-morning wakeup for Ninth Air Force B-26B-15-MA Marauder 41-31606 (fuselage code AN-S) of the 386th Bomb Group, 553rd Bomb Squadron, at Beaumont-sur-Oise Airfield (A-60). The ground crew have opened up the aircraft, and one man is getting ready to remove the cover over the Martin CE-250 gun turret (cylindrical, electric, 2 × 0.50-caliber machine guns) in the aft fuselage. This Marauder was delivered on March 15, 1943, and sent overseas under code Ugly A, departing on May 25, 1943, and arriving to serve with the Eighth Air Force in England three days later. Subsequently transferred to the Ninth Air Force, 41-31606 fought until the end of the war, was placed into storage, and was salvaged on March 14, 1946. NARA/USAAF 56355AC

Facing page bottom: Red nose P-51D of the 4th Fighter Group, 335th Fighter Squadron, carrying 108-gallon paper drop tanks, taxies out at USAAF Station 356, RAF Debden. At the controls of P-51D-5-NA 44-13883 (fuselage code WD-A) is Maj. Pierce W. "Mac" McKennon, who was shot down in this aircraft on August 28, 1944, near Strasbourg, France. McKennon was able to evade capture and return to Allied lines to fly again. McKennon's aircraft all wore the same fuselage code, and most of the planes he was assigned were named *Ridge Runner*.

The 4th Fighter Group flew five missions in support of the D-Day landings on June 6, the first taking off at 3:30 a.m. The group paid a high price for its missions that day. A number of patrols were met by superior German forces, and ten pilots from the group did not return. NARA/USAAF

The first Douglas Havoc in the European Theater to complete 100 missions was A-20G-25-DO 43-9224, *Miss Laid*. The bomber completed its centennial mission on June 6 and on that day was flown by Lt. Charles L. McGlohn. The aircraft never turned back, due to mechanical problems, and the engines that it arrived with were the ones that powered it over the Normandy beachhead on its hundredth mission. The crew chief responsible for *Miss Laid*'s care was T/Sgt. Royal S. Everts.

As the Allied armies pushed across France and toward Germany, a ceremony was held on October 27, 1944, at Le Bourget Airfield outside Paris. In addition to Technical Sergeant Everts, *Miss Laid*'s original crew of pilot Capt. Hugh A. Monroe (San Francisco, California) and S/Sgts. Wilmar L. Kidd (turret gunner; Neodesha, Kansas) and Steve Risko (gunner; Chicago, Illinois) were on hand. French actress Madame Monique Rolland rededicated the plane *La France Libre* to represent the goodwill between the United States and France. NARA/USAAF 54808AC

The Northrop P-61 Black Widow was the Army Air Forces' first purpose-built, radar-equipped night fighter. The Black Widow's introduction to combat in the European Theater came in the weeks following the D-Day landings. The twin-boom, twin-tail aircraft was powered by two Pratt & Whitney R-2800 engines. For night fighting, it was fitted with an SCR-720 radar (British nomenclature AI Mk X) that had a 15-mile range under ideal conditions.

Seen in formation are P-61-10-NO 42-5536, *Lovely Lady* (closest to camera); 42-5573, *Husslin' Hussey* (background); and 42-5564, *Jukin' Judy* (leading formation). Crews flying *Lovely Lady* were credited with downing two Ju 88 night intruders in August; by the end of the war, crews flying *Husslin' Hussey* had counted four confirmed kills, one probable, and one locomotive; *Jukin' Judy* (wearing eyes and a shark mouth) was responsible for downing an Fw 190. NARA/USAAF 53810AC AND 54955AC

Above: P-61A 42-5569, *Tabitha*, at Coulommiers, France. The airfield was a Luftwaffe base and was attacked by Eighth Air Force B-17s on June 14 and Ninth Air Force B-26s nine days later. On June 27, P-51 Mustangs strafed the airfield, hoping to destroy the Dornier Do 217N-2 and Messerschmitt Bf 110 night fighters stationed there.

Tabitha crashed on approach to land on October 24, 1944, killing her crew of Lt. Bruce Heflin and radar operator Lt. William B. Broach. NARA/USAAF A49481

Facing page top: Maintainers from the 425th Night Fighter Squadron, Cpl. Arthur Wilitscher of Brooklyn, New York, and Cpl. Roy Challberg of Rockford, Illinois, check the number-two propeller of P-61A-10-NO 42-5576, *Sleepy Time Gal*. This Black Widow arrived on June 24 and was flown by Capt. Earl W. "Bill" Bierer and radar operator Lt. James Lothrop. The night fighter's crew chief was Sgt. John W. Birmingham. NARA/USAAF 61362AC

Facing page bottom: P-61A-10-NO 42-5580, *Wabash Cannon-Ball IV*, from the 425th Night Fighter Squadron, is prepared for the evening's flight by crew chief T/Sgt. Neal C. Colbert of Lakeland, Florida (standing outside the aircraft) and mechanic Sgt. E. P. McSwain from York, South Carolina. The fuselage-mounted 20mm cannon are yet to be armed with the belts of ammunition on the ground beneath the aircraft's belly. The radar operator's hatch is open at the rear of the fuselage. The aircraft's name came from the 1936 Roy Acuff recording "Wabash Cannonball." NARA/USAAF 61362AC

Left: A ground crew member inspects P-61A-10-NO 42-5570, *Daisy Mae*, before a flight to combat German night fighters. *Daisy Mae* arrived with the 425th Night Fighter Squadron on June 26 at RAF Scorton. On August 18 the squadron moved to Maupertus Airfield (A-15) near Cherbourg, France. NARA/USAAF K2958

Below: PFC Cornelius Murphy of Hoboken, New Jersey (left) and Sgt. Robert Hendricks of San Francisco load 20mm ammunition into cans that will fly in P-61A-10-NO 42-5583, *Dangerous Dan*. The 425th Night Fighter Squadron Black Widow was assigned to Pilot Lt. Hugh Byars and radar operator Lt. Bob Brolik. *Dangerous Dan*'s crew chief was Sgt. Albert DiLorenzo. In November 1944, while being flown by a different crew, *Dangerous Dan* was shot down by flak near Saarbrücken, Germany. NARA/USAAF K2962

BUILDING AIRFIELDS

Above: The IX Engineer Command followed the initial waves ashore and completed a 3,600-foot dirt strip by 5:53 p.m. on Thursday, June 9. NARA/USAAF 51793AC

Left: Engineers deploy barrage balloons to help protect troops constructing an advance landing field, most likely Saint-Laurent-sur-Mer (A-21C) based on its proximity to the beaches in the background. The balloon is a British Mark VI kite balloon used to deter low-flying Luftwaffe aircraft from strafing the area. NARA/USAAF 52011AC

Left: Foliage was stripped from the ground, holes filled, and the ground leveled to convert former farmers' fields into emergency landing strips. NARA/USAAF 55173AC

Below: The IX Engineer Command's "Dozer Devils" prepare to start construction of an advanced landing field. Bulldozers, graders, DUKWs, and jeeps, seen in the background, were just a small sampling of the kit brought ashore by the engineers. NARA/ USAAF 51667AC

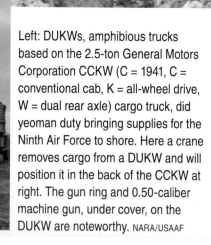

Left: DUKWs, amphibious trucks based on the 2.5-ton General Motors Corporation CCKW (C = 1941, C = conventional cab, K = all-wheel drive, W = dual rear axle) cargo truck, did yeoman duty bringing supplies for the Ninth Air Force to shore. Here a crane removes cargo from a DUKW and will position it in the back of the CCKW at right. The gun ring and 0.50-caliber machine gun, under cover, on the DUKW are noteworthy. NARA/USAAF

Top: Work on A-21C at Saint-Laurent-sur-Mer continues as bulldozers and earth scrapers change the former farming fields into a crash-landing strip. This enabled Allied pilots whose aircraft was too badly damaged to land safely rather than risk getting wet trying to cross the English Channel to safety. Here members of the 818th Engineer Aviation Battalion work while soldiers stay vigilant for German snipers. NARA/USAAF 51863AC

Bottom: A Stinson L-5-VW, 42-99328, has just taxied off the strip at Villacoublay. The strip was open for light aircraft while construction was being completed to accommodate larger aircraft. This field was liberated from the Luftwaffe on August 27, 1944, and immediately the IX Engineer Command's 818th Engineer Aviation Battalion set to work repairing the field and preparing it for Allied aircraft. The first tenant unit was the P-47–equipped 48th Fighter Group. NARA/USAAF 59202AC

Ninth Air Force Engineers roll out SMT, or square mesh track. SMT was ideal for building runways in a hurry, was lighter to transport than the more commonly seen PSP (pierced steel planking), and greater lengths of SMT could be transported in the same shipping space as PSP. SMT came in rolls 7 feet, 3 inches wide by 77 feet, 3 inches long, with each square 3 inches wide. The roll was unfurled, tacked down, and then the next roll staggered but overlapping the first roll by one or two squares. The overlapped mesh was then clipped together and staked to the ground. Overlapping and clips can be seen on the seam ahead of the road grader. Additional rolls have been delivered to continue the process. NARA/USAAF 52440AC, 51864AC, AND 52511AC

Airfield A-9 was built outside the village of Le Molay-Littry, approximately 7 miles (11 km) west of Bayeux, by the 834th Engineer Aviation Battalion. A-9 was operational on July 5, and soon after the F-5 Lightning and F-6 Mustang camera ships of the 10th Photo Reconnaissance Group arrived. Two large hangars were brought over and assembled on the field, making it one of the only airstrips with hangars in the Normandy region. With the battle moving forward at a rapid pace, the Allies did not need to build large hangars, as they were obtained when troops overran former Luftwaffe airfields. The hangar shown here was designed by the Butler Manufacturing Company of Kansas City, Missouri. The steel frames nested together for shipping and were assembled in small subassemblies, then erected in large segments. This model of the Butler hangars went up so fast because the time-consuming task of skinning the building was replaced by thick water- and fireproof canvas. The canvas panels were laced together and then suspended from the steel frame.

Le Molay-Littry (A-9) became an important airfield as General Eisenhower established a forward command post, code name "Shellburst," at nearby Tournières. NARA/USAAF 76674AC, A-76674AC, AND B-76674AC

When not building airfields, workers in this case a local French contractor were busy repairing bomb holes in runways and taxiways from the previous day's bombing by the Luftwaffe. Although the Allies had air superiority over the beachhead area, it was not complete, and the Luftwaffe was a force to be reckoned with. A 425th Night Fighter Squadron P-61 Black Widow can be seen running up in the background, while a Cessna UC-78 trainer sits at right. UC-78s were used by night fighter squadrons for base hack and training duties. NARA/USAAF B-61349AC

MAINTENANCE IN THE FIELD

Scratching his head as he realizes how lucky he is to be alive, Maj. Loren W. Herway, commanding officer of the 362nd Fighter Group's 377th Fighter Squadron, inspects the hole in his Thunderbolt's fuselage made by an 88mm shell. It was Herway's 124th mission, and with supercharger and hydraulics, as well as a damaged rudder, he was able to fly the stricken P-47 back to base, where he belly-landed the wreck. NARA/USAAF 56597AC

Left: Col. Ray J. Stecker, commanding officer of the 365th Fighter Group and former West Point All American softball star, and S/Sgt. Harry Greenwood discuss the fate of a 387th Fighter Squadron (fuselage code B4) Thunderbolt. The P-47 took a direct flak hit at low level but was able to make it back to advanced landing ground A-7 at Azeville. Damaged beyond repair, this Thunderbolt was stripped of useful parts and subsequently scrapped. NARA/USAAF 52853AC

Below: Members of the Ninth Air Force's Service Command Mobile Reclamation and Repair set up camp for an extended stay working to put this Martin B-26 Marauder back into fighting shape. Mobile Reclamation and Repair units were divided into small detachments, and each was self-sufficient. These units were a tremendous advantage to the Allies in keeping large numbers of aircraft fit for combat. NARA/USAAF 54531AC

Top: Lt. Gen. George S. Patton's Third Army received tremendous air support from the Ninth Air Force's XIX Tactical Air Command, led by Brig. Gen. Otto P. Weyland (second from left). Inspecting a P-51 Mustang with General Patton (at left) and General Weyland are Col. Homer Sanders (third from left), commander of the XIX Tactical Air Command's 100th Fighter Wing, and Col. George R. Bickell (at right), commanding officer of the 354th Fighter Group. Gen. Patton was expressing his appreciation to the airmen for their units' air support. NARA/USAAF 54541

Bottom: Maintenance area at an advance landing field near the French coast, with a mix of P-47s in various stages of repair and a P-51B in the left foreground. The P-47D in the foreground at right is from the 406th Fighter Group's 514th Fighter Squadron and wears the fuselage code O7-C. NARA/USAAF 53471

Top: Thunderbolts line an advance landing ground, possibly A-21C at Saint-Laurent-sur-Mer based on the lack of trees in the background. The aircraft in the foreground at right is having its eight 0.50-caliber machine guns reloaded as well as some maintenance work done in the engine accessory section. The variety of headgear is of interest—the aircraft maintainers are all wearing baseball-type caps; the GIs on and around the bomb truck sport steel helmets, with one having a knit cap. At left is John F. Thornell Jr's P-47D-2-RA 42-22474, *Pattie.* Thornell achieved "Ace" status by June 21, 1944, and amassed a total of 17.25 aerial victories over Bf 109s and Fw 190s as well as a shared credit for an Me 410 before the end of the war. NARA/USAAF

Bottom: The 367th Fighter Group flew both the P-38 and P-47. On D-Day and the subsequent two days, the 367th flew nine missions. On June 22, Allied aircraft attacked the Germans surrounding the port of Cherbourg with a dozen Ninth Air Force fighter groups. The fighters were to go in low in advance of the medium bombers, and the 367th was the last group over the target. By that time the Germans had found their range. Only eleven aircraft from the 367th Fighter Group returned without damage, and seven pilots were killed during this one mission. Hit by flak during a sortie over German lines, P-38J 42-104144 from the 367th Fighter Group, 392nd Fighter Squadron, was damaged beyond repair and is being stripped of usable parts before being scrapped. NARA/USAAF B-53740AC

Top: Not much remains of this 362nd Fighter Group, 378th Fighter Squadron P-47 (fuselage code G8-G) as maintainers strip the fuselage clean. Notice that the left wing is still attached to the fuselage, providing a main gear, while the right wing has been removed and a jack holds the aircraft up. Ducting for the turbosupercharger can be seen in the background under the tail, while a mechanic is removing items from behind the pilot's seat. Another is in the cockpit, while an additional pair work in the engine accessory section. Removing parts from a damaged aircraft to keep another fighting is a process that continues to this day, and in the early days of the invasion, before massive supplies made their way from the United States to Britain and on to France, reusing parts from one damaged aircraft was the only source of spares. NARA/USAAF A-53740

Bottom: Lt. Floyd Mills put his damaged Thunderbolt back on the field, but it was a write-off. The P-47, known as *The Mighty Mills*, served with the 362nd Fighter Group, 378th Fighter Squadron, and is seen on its belly at A-12, Lignerolles. Enemy troops must be near, as Pvt. Dioniclo D. Johnson, working on the starboard main landing gear, has a steel helmet and M1 carbine close at hand. On the far side of the fuselage, working on the engine mount, is Pvt. Emery Mcfain; in the cockpit is Cpl. Donald F. Condon. NARA/USAAF 11645AC

APPENDIX I

Operation Overlord Medal of Honor Recipients

The Medal of Honor is given to active-duty US servicemembers for conspicuous gallantry; it is America's oldest continuously awarded honor. President Abraham Lincoln signed Public Resolution 82 establishing the US Navy's Medal of Valor on December 21, 1861, "to be bestowed upon such petty officers, seamen, landsmen, and Marines as shall most distinguish themselves by their gallantry and other seamanlike qualities during the present war." In recognition of US Army soldiers who distinguished themselves on the battlefield, Lincoln soon after signed a resolution providing the Army Medal of Honor for "such noncommissioned officers and privates as shall most distinguish themselves by their gallantry in action, and other soldierlike qualities, during the present insurrection." In 1863 Congress combined the two services' medals into one and adopted the name Medal of Honor. In 1942 the medal's qualification criteria were changed, and the award was subsequently given for combat bravery only.

During World War II, 440 servicemen received the Medal of Honor, 250 of which were posthumously awarded. The Medal of Honor was awarded to 301 soldiers (US Army and Army Air Forces), 57 sailors, 81 Marines, and 1 Coast Guardsman. Twelve men were recognized for their bravery during Operation Overlord and in the subsequent battles to break out from the beachhead and begin the march to Germany.

Barrett, Carlton W.
Rank and Organization: Private, US Army, 18th Infantry, 1st Infantry Division
Place and date: Near St. Laurent-sur-Mer, France, June 6, 1944
Entered service at: Albany, New York
Birth: November 24, 1919, Fulton, New York
Died: May 3, 1986, Napa, California
Citation (October 2, 1944): For gallantry and intrepidity at the risk of his life above and beyond the call of duty on June 6, 1944, in the vicinity of St. Laurent-sur-Mer, France.

On the morning of D-Day Pvt. Barrett, landing in the face of extremely heavy enemy fire, was forced to wade ashore through neck-deep water. Disregarding the personal danger, he returned to the surf again and again to assist his floundering comrades and save them from drowning. Refusing to remain pinned down by the intense barrage of small-arms and mortar fire poured at the landing points, Pvt. Barrett, working with fierce determination, saved many lives by carrying casualties to an evacuation boat lying offshore.

In addition to his assigned mission as guide, he carried dispatches the length of the fire-swept beach; he assisted the wounded; he calmed the shocked; he arose as a leader in the stress of the occasion. His coolness and his dauntless daring courage while constantly risking his life during a period of many hours had an inestimable effect on his comrades and is in keeping with the highest traditions of the US Army.

Butts, John E.

Rank and Organization: Second Lieutenant, US Army, Co. E, 60th Infantry, 9th Infantry Division
Place and date: Normandy, France, June 14, 16, and 23, 1944
Entered service at: Buffalo, New York
Birth: August 4, 1922, Medina, New York
Citation (July 19, 1945; awarded posthumously): Heroically led his platoon against the enemy in Normandy, France, on June 14, 16, and 23, 1944. Although painfully wounded on June 14, near Orglandes, and again on June 16, while spearheading an attack to establish a bridgehead across the Douve River, he refused medical aid and remained with his platoon.

A week later, near Flottemanville-Hague, he led an assault on a tactically important and stubbornly defended hill studded with tanks, antitank guns, pillboxes, and machinegun emplacements, and protected by concentrated artillery and mortar fire. As the attack was launched, 2nd Lt. Butts, at the head of his platoon, was critically wounded by German machinegun fire. Although weakened by his injuries, he rallied his

men and directed one squad to make a flanking movement while he alone made a frontal assault to draw the hostile fire upon himself. Once more he was struck, but by grim determination and sheer courage continued to crawl ahead. When within 10 yards of his objective, he was killed by direct fire. By his superb courage, unflinching valor and inspiring actions, Second Lt. Butts enabled his platoon to take a formidable strong point and contributed greatly to the success of his battalion's mission.

DeGlopper, Charles N.

Rank and Organization: Private First Class, US Army, Co. C, 325th Glider Infantry, 82nd Airborne Division
Place and date: Merderet River at La Fiére, France, June 9, 1944
Entered service at: Grand Island, New York
Birth: November 30, 1921, Grand Island, New York
Citation (February 28, 1946; awarded posthumously): PFC DeGlopper was a member of Company C, 325th Glider Infantry, on June 9, 1944, advancing with the forward platoon to secure a bridgehead across the Merderet River at La Fiére, France. At dawn the platoon had penetrated an outer line of machine-guns and riflemen, but in so doing had become cut off from the rest of the company. Vastly superior forces began a decimation of the stricken unit and put in motion a flanking maneuver which would have completely exposed the American platoon in a shallow roadside ditch where it had taken cover. Detecting this danger, PFC DeGlopper volunteered to support his comrades by fire from his automatic rifle while they attempted a withdrawal through a break in a hedgerow 40 yards to the rear.

Scorning a concentration of enemy automatic weapons and rifle fire, he walked from the ditch onto the road in full view of the Germans, and sprayed the hostile positions with assault fire. He was wounded, but he continued firing. Struck again, he started to fall; and yet his grim determination and valiant fighting spirit could not be broken. Kneeling in the roadway, weakened by his grievous wounds, he leveled his heavy weapon against the enemy and fired burst after burst until killed outright.

He was successful in drawing the enemy action away from his fellow soldiers, who continued the fight from a more advantageous position and established the first bridgehead over the Merderet River. In the area where he made his intrepid stand his comrades later found the ground strewn with dead Germans and many machineguns and automatic weapons which he had knocked out of action. PFC DeGlopper's gallant sacrifice and unflinching heroism while facing unsurmountable odds were in great measure responsible for a highly important tactical victory in the Normandy Campaign.

Ehlers, Walter D.

Rank and organization: Staff Sergeant, US Army, 18th Infantry, 1st Infantry Division
Place and date: Near Goville, France, June 9–10, 1944
Entered service at: Manhattan, Kansas
Birth: May 7, 1921, Junction City, Kansas
Died: February 20, 2014, Long Beach, California
Citation (December 19, 1944): For conspicuous gallantry and intrepidity at the risk of his life above and beyond the call of duty on June 9–10, 1944, near Goville, France. S/Sgt. Ehlers, always acting as the spearhead of the attack, repeatedly led his men against heavily defended enemy strong points, exposing himself to deadly hostile fire whenever the situation required heroic and courageous

leadership. Without waiting for an order, S/Sgt. Ehlers, far ahead of his men, led his squad against a strongly defended enemy strong point, personally killing four of an enemy patrol who attacked him en route. Then crawling forward under withering machinegun fire, he pounced upon the guncrew and put it out of action.

Turning his attention to two mortars protected by the crossfire of two machineguns, S/Sgt. Ehlers led his men through this hail of bullets to kill or put to flight the enemy of the mortar section, killing three men himself. After mopping up the mortar positions, he again advanced on a machinegun, his progress effectively covered by his squad. When he was almost on top of the gun he leaped to his feet and, although greatly outnumbered, he knocked out the position single-handed.

The next day, having advanced deep into enemy territory, the platoon of which S/Sgt. Ehlers was a member, finding itself in an untenable position as the enemy brought increased mortar, machinegun, and small arms fire to bear on it, was ordered to withdraw. S/Sgt. Ehlers, after his squad had covered the withdrawal of the remainder of the platoon, stood up and by continuous fire at the semicircle of enemy placements, diverted the bulk of the heavy hostile fire on himself, thus permitting the members of his own squad to withdraw. At this point, though wounded himself, he carried his wounded automatic rifleman to safety and then returned fearlessly over the shell-swept field to retrieve the automatic rifle which he was unable to carry previously.

After having his wound treated, he refused to be evacuated, and returned to lead his squad. The intrepid leadership, indomitable courage, and fearless aggressiveness displayed by S/Sgt. Ehlers in the face of overwhelming enemy forces serve as an inspiration to others.

Cole, Robert G.

Rank and organization: Lieutenant Colonel, US Army, 101st Airborne Division

Place and date: Near Carentan, France, June 11, 1944

Entered service at: San Antonio, Texas

Birth: March 19, 1915, Fort Sam Houston, Texas

Citation (October 4, 1944; awarded posthumously): For gallantry and intrepidity at the risk of his own life, above and beyond the call of duty, on June 11, 1944, in France. Lt. Col. Cole was personally leading his battalion in forcing the last four bridges on the road to Carentan when his entire unit was suddenly pinned to the ground by intense and withering enemy rifle, machinegun, mortar, and artillery fire placed upon them from well-prepared and heavily fortified positions within 150 yards of the foremost elements.

After the devastating and unceasing enemy fire had for over one hour prevented any move and inflicted numerous casualties, Lt. Col. Cole, observing this almost hopeless situation, courageously issued orders to assault the enemy positions with fixed bayonets. With utter disregard for his own safety and completely ignoring the enemy fire, he rose to his feet in front of his battalion and with drawn pistol shouted to his men to follow him in the assault. Catching up a fallen man's rifle and bayonet, he charged on and led the remnants of his battalion across the bullet-swept open ground and into the enemy position. His heroic and valiant action in so inspiring his men resulted in the complete establishment of our bridgehead across the Douve River.

The cool fearlessness, personal bravery, and outstanding leadership displayed by Lt. Col. Cole reflect great credit upon himself and are worthy of the highest praise in the military service.

DeFranzo, Arthur F.

Rank and organization: Staff Sergeant, US Army, 1st Infantry Division

Place and date: Near Vaubadon, France, June 10, 1944

Entered service at: Saugus, Massachusetts

Birth: March 20, 1919, Saugus, Massachusetts

Citation (January 4, 1945; awarded posthumously): For conspicuous gallantry and intrepidity at the risk of his life, above and beyond the call of duty, on June 10, 1944, near Vaubadon, France.

As scouts were advancing across an open field, the enemy suddenly opened fire with several machineguns and hit one of the men. S/Sgt. DeFranzo courageously moved out in the open to the aid of the wounded scout and was himself wounded but brought the man to safety. Refusing aid, S/Sgt. DeFranzo reentered the open field and led the advance upon the enemy. There were always at least two machineguns bringing unrelenting fire upon him, but S/Sgt. DeFranzo kept going forward, firing into the enemy, and one by one the enemy emplacements became silent.

While advancing he was again wounded, but continued on until he was within 100 yards of the enemy position, and even as he fell, he kept firing his rifle and waving his men forward. When his company came up behind him, S/Sgt. DeFranzo, despite his many severe wounds, suddenly raised himself and once more moved forward in the lead of his men until he was again hit by enemy fire. In a final gesture of indomitable courage, he threw several grenades at the enemy machinegun position and completely destroyed the gun.

In this action, S/Sgt. DeFranzo lost his life, but by bearing the brunt of the enemy fire in leading the attack, he prevented a delay in the assault which would have been of considerable benefit to the foe, and he made possible his company's advance with a minimum of casualties.

The extraordinary heroism and magnificent devotion to duty displayed by S/Sgt. DeFranzo was a great inspiration to all about him, and is in keeping with the highest traditions of the armed forces.

Kelly, John D.

Rank and organization: Technical Sergeant (then Corporal), US Army, Company E, 314th Infantry, 79th Infantry Division

Place and date: Fort du Roule, Cherbourg, France, June 25, 1944

Entered service at: Cambridge Springs, Pennsylvania

Birth: July 8, 1923, Venango Township, Pennsylvania

Citation (January 24, 1945; awarded posthumously): For conspicuous gallantry and intrepidity at the risk of his life above and beyond the call of duty. On June 25, 1944, in the vicinity of Fort du Roule, Cherbourg, France, when Cpl. Kelly's unit was pinned down by heavy enemy machinegun fire emanating from a deeply entrenched strongpoint on the slope leading up to the fort, Cpl. Kelly volunteered to attempt to neutralize the strongpoint. Arming himself with a pole charge about 10 feet long and with 15 pounds of explosive affixed, he climbed the slope under a withering blast of machinegun fire and placed the charge at the strongpoint's base. The subsequent blast was ineffective, and again, alone and unhesitatingly, he braved the slope to repeat the operation. This second blast blew off the ends of the enemy guns. Cpl. Kelly then climbed the slope a third time to place a pole charge at the strongpoint's rear entrance. When this had been blown open he hurled hand grenades inside the position, forcing survivors of the enemy gun crews to come out and surrender.

The gallantry, tenacity of purpose, and utter disregard for personal safety displayed by Cpl. Kelly were an incentive to his comrades and worthy of emulation by all.

Monteith, Jimmie W., Jr.

Rank and organization: First Lieutenant, US Army, 16th Infantry, 1st Infantry Division

Place and date: Near Colleville-sur-Mer, France, June 6, 1944

Entered service at: Richmond, Virginia

Birth: July 1, 1917, Low Moor, Virginia

Citation (March 29, 1945; awarded posthumously): For conspicuous gallantry and intrepidity above and beyond the call of duty on June 6, 1944, near Colleville-sur-Mer, France.

First Lt. Monteith landed with the initial assault waves on the coast of France under heavy enemy fire. Without regard to his own personal safety he continually moved up and down the beach reorganizing men for further assault. He then led the assault over a narrow protective ledge and across the flat, exposed terrain to the comparative safety of a cliff.

Retracing his steps across the field to the beach, he moved over to where two tanks were buttoned up and blind under violent enemy artillery and machinegun fire. Completely exposed to the intense fire, First Lt. Monteith led the tanks on foot through a minefield and into firing positions. Under his direction several enemy positions were destroyed. He then rejoined his company and under his leadership his men captured an advantageous position on the hill. Supervising the defense of his newly won position against repeated vicious counterattacks, he continued to ignore his own personal safety, repeatedly crossing the 200 or 300 yards of open terrain under heavy fire to strengthen links in his defensive chain. When the enemy succeeded in completely surrounding First Lt. Monteith and his unit and while leading the fight out of the situation, First Lt. Monteith was killed by enemy fire. The courage, gallantry, and intrepid leadership displayed by First Lt. Monteith is worthy of emulation.

Ogden, Carlos C.

Rank and organization: First Lieutenant, US Army, Company K, 314th Infantry, 79th Infantry Division
Place and date: Near Fort du Roule, France, June 25, 1944
Entered service at: Fairmont, Illinois
Birth: May 19, 1917, Borton, Illinois
Died: April 2, 2001, Palo Alto, California
Citation (June 28, 1945): On the morning of June 25, 1944, near Fort du Roule, guarding the approaches to Cherbourg, France, First Lt. Ogden's company was pinned down by fire from a German 88mm gun and two machineguns. Arming himself with an M-1 rifle, a grenade launcher, and a number of rifle and hand grenades, he left his company in position and advanced alone, under fire, up the slope toward the enemy emplacements. Struck on the head and knocked down by a glancing machinegun bullet, 1st Lt. Ogden, in spite of his painful wound and enemy fire from close range, continued up the hill. Reaching a vantage point, he silenced the 88mm gun with a well-placed rifle grenade and then, with hand grenades, knocked out the two machineguns, again being painfully wounded.

First Lt. Ogden's heroic leadership and indomitable courage in alone silencing these enemy weapons inspired his men to greater effort and cleared the way for the company to continue the advance and reach its objectives.

Peregory, Frank D.

Rank and organization: Technical Sergeant, US Army, Company K, 116th Infantry, 29th Infantry Division

Place and date: Grandcampe, France, June 8, 1944
Entered service at: Charlottesville, Virginia
Born: April 10, 1915, Esmont, Virginia
Citation (May 30, 1945; awarded posthumously): On June 8, 1944, the 3rd Battalion of the 116th Infantry was advancing on the strongly held German defenses at Grandcampe, France, when the leading elements were suddenly halted by decimating machinegun fire from a firmly entrenched enemy force on the high ground overlooking the town. After numerous attempts to neutralize the enemy position by supporting artillery and tank fire had proved ineffective, T/Sgt. Peregory, on his own initiative, advanced up the hill under withering fire, and worked his way to the crest where he discovered an entrenchment leading to the main enemy fortifications 200 yards away. Without hesitating, he leaped into the trench and moved toward the emplacement. Encountering a squad of enemy riflemen, he fearlessly attacked them with hand grenades and bayonet, killed 8 and forced 3 to surrender. Continuing along the trench, he single-handedly forced the surrender of 32 more riflemen, captured the machine gunners, and opened the way for the leading elements of the battalion to advance and secure its objective. The extraordinary gallantry and aggressiveness displayed by T/Sgt. Peregory are exemplary of the highest tradition of the armed forces.

Pinder, John J., Jr.

Rank and organization: Technician Fifth Grade, US Army, 16th Infantry, 1st Infantry Division
Place and date: Near Colleville-sur-Mer, France, June 6, 1944
Entered Service at: Burgettstown, Pennsylvania

Birth: June 6, 1912, McKees Rocks, Pennsylvania

Citation (January 4, 1945; awarded posthumously): For conspicuous gallantry and intrepidity above and beyond the call of duty on June 6, 1944, near Colleville-sur-Mer, France. On D-day, Technician Fifth Grade Pinder landed on the coast 100 yards offshore under devastating enemy machinegun and artillery fire which caused severe casualties among the boatload.

Carrying a vitally important radio, he struggled towards shore in waist-deep water. Only a few yards from his craft he was hit by enemy fire and was gravely wounded. Technician Fifth Grade Pinder never stopped. He made shore and delivered the radio. Refusing to take cover afforded, or to accept medical attention for his wounds, Technician Fifth Grade Pinder, though terribly weakened by loss of blood and in fierce pain, on three occasions went into the fire-swept surf to salvage communication equipment. He recovered many vital parts and equipment, including another workable radio.

On the third trip he was again hit, suffering machinegun bullet wounds in the legs. Still this valiant soldier would not stop for rest or medical attention. Remaining exposed to heavy enemy fire, growing steadily weaker, he aided in establishing the vital radio communication on the beach. While so engaged this dauntless soldier was hit for the third time and killed. The indomitable courage and personal bravery of Technician Fifth Grade Pinder was a magnificent inspiration to the men with whom he served.

Roosevelt, Theodore, Jr.

Rank and organization: Brigadier General, US Army

Place and date: Normandy invasion, June 6, 1944

Entered service at: Oyster Bay, New York

Birth: September 13, 1887, Oyster Bay, New York

Citation (September 28, 1944; awarded posthumously): For gallantry and intrepidity at the risk of his life above and beyond the call of duty on June 6, 1944, in France. After two verbal requests to accompany the leading assault elements in the Normandy invasion had been denied, Brig. Gen. Roosevelt's written request for this mission was approved and he landed with the first wave of the forces assaulting the enemy-held beaches.

He repeatedly led groups from the beach, over the seawall and established them inland. His valor, courage, and presence in the very front of the attack and his complete unconcern at being under heavy fire inspired the troops to heights of enthusiasm and self-sacrifice.

Although the enemy had the beach under constant direct fire, Brig. Gen. Roosevelt moved from one locality to another, rallying men around him, directed and personally led them against the enemy. Under his seasoned, precise, calm, and unfaltering leadership, assault troops reduced beach strong points and rapidly moved inland with minimum casualties. He thus contributed substantially to the successful establishment of the beachhead in France.

Source: US Army Center of Military History (Normandy Invasion, Medal of Honor Recipients) with additions by the author: https://history.army.mil/html/reference/Normandy/nor-moh.html

APPENDIX II

Invasion Beach Airfields (June 6– September 4, 1944)

As the Allies moved off the beaches and into the interior of France, airfields were being constructed as ground was captured. This enabled tactical and reconnaissance aircraft to be moved forward from bases in England, reducing transit time across the English Channel while increasing time over the target.

American
Identity Location

A-1	Saint-Pierre-du-Mont
A-2	Cricqueville
A-3	Cardonville
A-4	Deux-Jumeaux
A-5	Chippelle
A-7	Azeville
A-8	Picauville
A-9	Le Molay
A-10	Carentan
A-11	Saint-Lambert
A-12	Lignerolles
A-13	Tour-en-Bessin
A-14	Cretteville
A-15	Maupertus
A-16	Brucheville
A-17	Méautis
A-18	Saint-Jean-de-Daye
A-19	La Vieille
A-20	Lessay
A-21C	Saint-Laurent-sur-Mer
A-22C	Colleville
A-23C	Querqueville
A-24C	Biniville
A-25C	Bolleville
A-26	Gorges
A-27	Rennes
A-28	Pontorson
A-29	Saint-James
A-30C	Courtils
A-31	Gaël
A-33N	Vannes
A-34	Gorron
A-35	Le Mans
A-36	Saint-Léonard
A-39	Châteaudun
A-40D	Chartres
A-41	Dreux
A-42D	Villacoublay
A-43	Saint-Marceau
A-44	Peray
A-46	Toussus-le-Noble
A-48	Brétigny
A-61	Beauvais (also known as B-40)

British

Identity Location

B-2	Bazenville
B-3	Sainte-Croix-sur-Mer
B-4	Bény-sur-Mer
B-5	Camilly
B-6	Coulombs
B-7	Martragny
B-8	Sommervieu
B-9	Lantheuil
B-10	Plumetot
B-11	Longues-sur-Mer
B-12	Ellon
B-14	Amblie
B-15	Ryes
B-16	Villons-les-Buissons
B-17	Carpiquet
B-18	Cristot
B-19	Lingèvres
B-21	Sainte-Honorine-de-Ducy
B-23	La Rue Huguenot
B-24	Saint-André-de-l'Eure
B-26	Illiers-l'Évêque
B-27	Boisney
B-28	Évreux
B-29	Valailles
B-30	Créton
B-33	Campneuseville
B-34	Avrilly
B-40	Beauvais (also known as A-61)
B-48	Amiens-Glisy

The first aircraft to land on an airstrip on the continent was this C-47, touching down at A-21C Saint-Laurent-sur-Mer, which was situated less than 1 mile inland from the water's edge. Built by the IX Engineer Command's 834th Engineer Aviation Battalion, this field was open on June 7 and was in use until July 16, 1944. C-47s were able to evacuate wounded soldiers from the area back to hospitals in England for immediate medical attention. USAAF 51670AC

APPENDIX III

Ship Losses, Normandy Invasion (June 6–25, 1944)

Ship	Status; Date; Cause
Destroyer (DD)	
Corry (DD-463)	Lost; June 6, 1944; shore battery
Glennon (DD-620)	Lost; June 8, 1944; mine
Meredith (DD-726)	Lost; June 7, 1944; mine
Nelson (DD-623)	Damaged June 13, 1944; E-boat torpedo
Destroyer Escort (DE)	
Rich (DE-695)	Lost; June 8, 1944; shore battery
Minesweeper (AM)	
Osprey (AM-56)	Lost; June 5, 1944; mine
Tide (AM-125)	Lost; June 7, 1944; mine
Patrol Craft (PC)	
PC-1261	Lost; June 6, 1944; shore battery (primary control vessel, Utah Beach, Red Sector)
District Motor Minesweeper (YMS)	
YMS-406	Damaged
Motor Torpedo Boat (PT)	
PT-505	Damaged; June 7, 1944; mine
Transport (AP)	
Susan B. Anthony	Lost; June 7, 1944; mine
Ocean Tug (AT[O])	
Partridge (AT[O]-138)	Lost; June 11, 1944; E-boat torpedo

Landing Craft, Control (LCC)

LCC-80	Damaged (secondary control vessel for Utah Beach, Red Sector)

Landing Ship, Tank (LST)

LST-314	Lost; June 9, 1944; E-boat torpedo
LST-375	Damaged
LST-376	Lost; June 9, 1944; E-boat torpedo
LST-496	Lost; June 11, 1944; E-boat torpedo
LST-499	Lost; June 8, 1944
LST-536	Damaged
LST-543	Damaged

(plus twenty-five others damaged)

Landing Craft, Infantry, Large (LCI[L])

LCI(L)-85	Lost; June 6, 1944; mine and shore battery fire
LCI(L)-87	Damaged
LCI(L)-88	Damaged
LCI(L)-91	Lost; June 6, 1944; shore battery fire, Omaha/Easy Red Beach
LCI(L)-92	Lost; June 6, 1944; mines, shore battery fire, Omaha/Easy Green Beach
LCI(L)-93	Lost; June 6, 1944; shore battery fire, Omaha/Easy Red Beach
LCI(L)-209	Damaged
LCI(L)-212	Damaged
LCI(L)-219	Lost; June 11, 1944
LCI(L)-416	Lost; June 6, 1944; mine
LCI(L)-497	Lost; June 6, 1944; mine
LCI(L)-553	Lost; June 6, 1944; shore battery fire

(plus eighty-three others damaged)

Landing Craft, Flak (LCF)

LCF-31	Lost; June 6, 1944; shore battery fire

LCT(4) (Landing Craft, Tank [Mark IV])

LCT(4)-690	Damaged
LCT(4)-875	Lost
LCT(4)-921	Damaged
LCT(4)-967	Lost
LCT(4)-1035	Damaged
LCT(4)-1037	Damaged
LCT(4)-1124	Damaged (delivered too late for D-Day)

LCT(5) (Landing Craft, Tank [Mark V]; Armored [A])

LCT(5)-25	Lost; June 6, 1944
LCT(5)-27	Lost; June 6, 1944; grounded
LCT(5)-29	Damaged
LCT(5)-30	Lost; June 6, 1944; mine

LCT(5)-149	Damaged
LCT(5)-197	Lost; June 6, 1944; mine
LCT(5)-200	Lost; June 6, 1944
LCT(5)-201	Damaged
LCT(5)-210	Damaged
LCT(5)-213	Damaged
LCT(5)-294	Lost; June 6, 1944; mine
LCT(5)-305	Lost; June 6, 1944
LCT(5)-332	Lost; June 6, 1944; mine
LCT(5)-362	Lost; June 6, 1944; swamped, Utah/Uncle Red Beach
LCT(5)-364	Lost; June 6, 1944; mine
LCT(5)-397	Damaged
LCT(5)-458	Lost; June 6, 1944; mine
LCT(5)-460	Damaged; June 6, 1944
LCT(5)-486	Lost; June 6, 1944; shore battery fire, Utah/Tare Green Beach
LCT(5)-2049	Lost; June 6, 1944
LCT(5)-2287	Damaged
LCT(5)-2297	Damaged
LCT(5)-2307	Lost; June 6, 1944
LCT(5)-2425	Damaged
LCT(5)-2485	Damaged
LCT(A)-2498	Lost; June 6, 1944

LCT(6) (Landing Craft, Tank [Mark VI])

LCT(6)-515	Damaged
LCT(6)-522	Damaged
LCT(6)-524	Damaged
LCT(6)-527	Damaged
LCT(6)-528	Damaged
LCT(6)-538	Damaged
LCT(6)-540	Lost; June 6, 1944
LCT(6)-541	Damaged
LCT(6)-543	Damaged
LCT(6)-555	Damaged
LCT(6)-516	Damaged
LCT(6)-572	Damaged
LCT(6)-581	Damaged
LCT(6)-593	Lost; June 6, 1944; mine
LCT(6)-597	Lost; June 6, 1944; mine
LCT(6)-612	Damaged
LCT(6)-637	Damaged
LCT(6)-650	Damaged
LCT(6)-665	Lost; June 6, 1944
LCT(6)-703	Lost; June 6, 1944; mine
LCT(6)-711	Damaged
LCT(6)-714	Lost; June 6, 1944
LCT(6)-715	Damaged

LCT(6)-767	Damaged
LCT(6)-777	Lost; June 6, 1944; mine
LCT(6)-856	Lost; June 6, 1944

Landing Craft, Tank (Armored) (LCT[A])

LCT(A)-2008	Damaged
LCT(A)-2037	Damaged
LCT(A)-2043	Damaged
LCT(A)-2124	Damaged
LCT(A)-2227	Damaged
LCT(A)-2273	Damaged
LCT(A)-2275	Damaged
LCT(A)-2402	Damaged

Landing Craft, Mechanized, Mark III (LCM[3])
Eight lost on Omaha Beach

Landing Craft, Support (Small) (LCS[S])
One lost on Omaha Beach

Landing Craft, Vehicle, Personnel (LCVP)
Twenty-six lost on Utah Beach
Fifty-five lost on Omaha Beach

Landing Craft, Assault (LCA)
Seventeen lost on Utah Beach

LCP(L) Smokers
Seven lost on Utah Beach

Royal Navy Ships

HMS *Minister* (trawler)	Lost
HM Seaplane Tender 350	Lost

Minesweeper (MS)

HMS *Kellett* (J 05)	Damaged
HMS *Tadoussac* (J 220)	Damaged

Motor Minesweeper (MMS)

MMS-229	Lost

Dan Layer

HMS *Peterhead* (J 59)	Lost; June 8, 1944; mine

Source: Naval Commander Western Task Force. *Report of Sunk and Damaged Ships and Craft.* June 17, 1944. (Document supplemented with additions by the author.)

APPENDIX IV

Allied Aircraft Losses (June 5/6–June 7/8, 1944)

Ninth Air Force P-47D-30-RE 42-26136, from the 373rd Fighter Group, 410th Fighter Squadron (fuselage code R3-J), made a forced landing on Utah Beach on June 14. The pilot was returned to service immediately, thus no Missing Air Crew Report was filed. The Thunderbolt was stripped of usable parts and subsequently scrapped. NARA

Eighth Air Force

Type	Serial	Pilot	Group	Squadron	Target/Area	Crew Status
June 5/6						
B-24D-1-CF	42-63784	1st Lt. K. Pratt	801 BG	36 BS	SOE, Belgium-Luxembourg	5 KIA, 2 POW, 1 Evaded
June 6						
B-24H-15-FO	42-52629	2nd Lt. N. E. Gross	487 BG	838 BS	Caen, France	10 KIA
B-24H-15-FO	42-94789	1st Lt. D. L. Russell	493 BG	862 BS	Lisieux, France	10 KIA
B-24J-165-CO	44-40471	Capt. J. G. W. Cooper	493 BG	863 BS	Lisieux, France	10 KIA
P-47D-22-RE	42-25963	2nd Lt. E. D. McMinn	56 FG	61 FS	Bernay, France	1 KIA
P-47D-20-RE	42-25578	2nd Lt. W. R. Hailey	78 FG	84 FS	Chaillons-Coulonche, France	English Channel, Rescued
P-47D-11-RE	42-75552	F/O E. W. Green	353 FG	352 FS	Mortain, France	POW
P-47D-22-RE	42-25997	F/O E. F. Sova	356 FG	360 FS	Le Mans, France	POW
P-47D-15-RE	42-75625	2nd Lt. G. C. Kariva	356 FG	360 FS	St. Omer, France	English Channel, POW
P-51C-1-NT	42-103287	1st Lt. H. H. Frederick	4 FG	336 FS	Calleville, France	Evaded
P-51C-5-NT	42-103332	1st Lt. O. F. Lajeunesse	4 FG	336 FS	Pont-Saint-Pierre, France	POW
P-51B-10-NA	42-106576	Capt. B. L. McGrattan	4 FG	335 FS	Le Neubourg, France	KIA
P-51B-10-NA	42-106786	1st Lt. H. L. Ross Jr.	4 FG	335 FS	Le Neubourg, France	KIA
P-51B-5-NA	43-6575	2nd Lt. C. E. Garbey	4 FG	335 FS	Le Neubourg, France	KIA
P-51B-5-NA	43-6898	Maj. W. M. Sobanski	4 FG	334 FS	Normanville, France	KIA
P-51B-5-NA	43-6957	2nd Lt. E. J. Steppe	4 FG	334 FS	Évreux, France	KIA
P-51B-10-NA	43-7172	F/O W. Smith Jr.	4 FG	335 FS	Le Neubourg, France	KIA
P-51B-15-NA	43-24825	2nd Lt. T. E. Fraser	4 FG	334 FS	Cambrai-Niergnies Airfield, France	POW
P-51B-15-NA	42-106909	Maj. M. G. H. McPharlin	4 FG	334 FS	Le Buisson Isabelle, France	KIA
P-51B-10-NA	42-106449	1st Lt. R. K. Butler	352 FG	487 FS	Pont-Audemer, France	Evaded
P-51B-5-NA	43-7096	1st Lt. R. G. O'Nan	352 FG	487 FS	Beaumont-le-Roger Airfield, France	POW
P-51B-15-NA	42-106862	2nd Lt. W. A. Douglass	355 FG	357 FS	Saint-Pol, France	POW
P-51B-5-NA	43-6640	1st Lt. G. W. Phillips	355 FG	357 FS	Villequier, France	KIA

Eighth Air Force

Type	Serial	Pilot	Group	Squadron	Target/Area	Crew Status
June 6						
P-51B-15-NA	42-106768	Capt. L. A. Ruder	357 FG	364 FS	Lannion, France	KIA
P-51B-5-NA	43-6397	1st Lt. R. E. Pagels	357 FG	363 FS	Isle of Guernsey, France	Evaded
P-51B-5-NA	43-6947	1st Lt. I. A. Smith	357 FG	363 FS	Nantes, France	KIA
P-51C-5-NT	42-103347	1st Lt. L. B. Perry	361 FG	375 FS	Coudres, France	KIA
P-51B-10-NA	42-106651	2nd Lt. W. D. Willett	361 FG	376 FS	Mondoubleau, France	POW
P-51B-5-NA	43-6977	2nd Lt. J. R. Golden	361 FG	374 FS	Forges-les-Eaux, France	POW
F-5C-1-LO	42-67246	1st Lt. J. E. Wicker	7 PRG	22 PRS	Châteaudun, France	POW
Other Losses						
B-24D-40-CO	44-40247	1st Lt. M. V. Courtney	389 BG	566 BS	Crashed during form-up	10 Killed
B-24H-15-DT	41-28838	2nd Lt. H. M. Doell	34 BG	7 BS	Crashed during form-up	10 Killed
B-17G-1-BO	42-31104	2nd Lt. G. L. Carter	477 BG	708 BS	Crashed on landing, Rattlesden	10 returned to service
B-17G-55-BO	42-102591	2nd Lt. P. A. Chase	447 BS	708 BS	Landed long, Rattlesden, hit 42-31104	10 Returned to service
B-24H-20-FO	42-94884	1st Lt. H. G. Hollan	490 BG	848 BS	Wet runway and crosswind	10 Returned to service
B-24H-20-FO	42-94885	1st Lt. D. G. McAusland	490 BG	850 BS	Landed on beach, English coast	4 KIA, 6 returned to service
B-24H-20-FO	42-94899	1st Lt. G. F. Gorgol	490 BG	848 BS	Off end of runway at Eye	9 Returned to service
P-38J-15-LO	43-28385	Maj. G. S. Wemyes	20 FG	77 FS	Landed short at King's Cliffe	Returned to service
P-51B-5-NA	43-6685	Lt. R. C. Frascotti	352 FG	486 FS	Takeoff accident at Bodney	1 Killed
Write-offs						
F-5B-1-LO	42-67334					
F-5B-1-LO	42-67343					
P-47D-21-RA	43-25555					
P-47D-21-RA	43-25538					
P-51B-10-NA	42-106579					
P-51B-15-NA	42-106928					
P-51B-5-NA	43-6781					
UC-61A-FA	43-14838					

June 7

Type	Serial	Name	Group	Squadron	Location	Fate
B-17G-45-BO	42-97238	Lt. J. A. Martyniak	381 BG	534 BS	Flak damage, ditched near Jersey	9 Rescued
B-24H-10-FO	42-52624	2nd Lt. F. Schwab	487 BG	839 BS	Rennes, France	7 KIA, 3 POW
P-47D-22-RE	42-26274	1st Lt. D. J. Furlong	56 FG	62 FS	Saint-Quentin-des-Prés, France	KIA
P-47D-22-RE	42-26342	1st Lt. W. A. McClure	56 FG	62 FS	Near Beauvais, France	Evaded
P-47D-15-RE	42-76254	2nd Lt. E. E. Bennett	56 FG	62 FS	Orbec, France	Evaded
P-47D-20-RA	43-25286	1st Lt. H. F. Warner Jr.	56 FG	63 FS	Liancourt-Saint-Pierre, France	KIA
P-47D-22-RE	42-25712	1st Lt. H. H. Just Jr.	78 FG	84 FS	Plainville, France	KIA
P-47D-15-RE	42-76184	1st Lt. H. H. Rice Jr.	78 FG	84 FS	Broyes, France	POW
P-47D-15-RE	42-76195	2nd Lt. L. Avakian	353 FG	352 FS	Meulers, France	KIA
P-47D-5-RE	42-8515	Capt. F. T. Walsh	353 FG	350 FS	Framicourt, France	KIA
P-47D-11-RE	42-75570	1st Lt. H. K. Field	353 FG	351 FS	Beauvais, France; English Channel	KIA
P-51B-5-NA	43-7042	1st Lt. O. R. Jones	4 FG	335 FS	Juilley, France	POW
P-51B-10-NA	42-106661	Maj. E. J. Gignac	352 FG	HQ Sqn	Versailles, France	KIA
P-51B-15-NA	43-24845	2nd Lt. Robert L. Hall	352 FG	487 FS	Argentan, France	KIA
P-51B-15-NA	42-106742	2nd Lt. T. J. Foster	355 FG	357 FS	Aunay-sous-Auneau, France	KIA
P-51B-15-NA	42-106810	2nd Lt. J. Guerrant Jr.	355 FG	357 FS	Saint-Riquier-ès-Plains, France	KIA
P-51B-5-NA	43-6886	2nd Lt. H. M. Harrell	355 FG	357 FS	Auneau, France	Evaded
P-51B-5-NA	43-6895	2nd Lt. R. D. Couture	355 FG	354 FS	Margon, France	Evaded
P-51B-5-NA	43-6916	2nd Lt. N. E. Hollman Jr.	355 FG	357 FS	Saint-Ange-et-Torçay, France	KIA
P-51B-5-NA	43-7039	1st Lt. W. E. MacFarlane	355 FG	357 FS	Houdan, France	POW
P-51B-10-NA	42-106652	2nd Lt. J. N. Denesha	357 FG	364 FS	Plancoët, France	KIA
P-51B-10-NA	42-106667	2nd Lt. J. C. Marcinkiewicz	359 FG	368 FS	Cap-d'Antifer, France	POW
P-51B-15-NA	42-106835	Maj. G. L. Merritt Jr.	361 FG	375 FS	Roiffé, France	KIA
P-51D-5-NA	44-13300	Maj. J. A. Goodson	4 FG	336 FS	Flak, Rennes, France; crashed RAF Merston	Returned to service

Other Losses

Type	Serial	Name	Group	Squadron	Location	Fate
B-24H-25-DT	42-51116	2nd Lt. R. Zeller	446 BG	705 BS	Corner Farm, Rumburgh, Suffolk	8 Killed, 4 returned to service
B-24H-15-CF	41-29572	2nd Lt. S. M. Brain	34 BG	18 BS	Shot down in pattern by Ju 88s	3 Killed, 7 returned to service
B-24H-15-FO	42-52696	1st Lt. O. T. Hanson	34 BG	391 BS	Shot down in pattern by Ju 88s	9 Returned to service

Type	Serial	Pilot	Group	Squadron	Target/Area	Crew Status
Eighth Air Force						
June 7						
B-24H-15-FO	42-52738	2nd Lt. H. D. Eastman	34 BG	391 BS	Shot down in pattern by Ju 88s	7 Killed
B-24H-20-FO	42-94911	2nd Lt. W. J. Dreher	34 BG	4 BS	Shot down in pattern by Ju 88s	3 Killed, 7 returned to service
P-51B-10-NA	42-106673	2nd Lt. K. D. Smith	4 FG	336 FS	Midair with 43-6714	Killed
P-51B-5-NA	43-6714	F/O D. J. Pierini	4 FG	336 FS	Midair with 42-106673	Returned to service
P-51C-5-NT	42-103341	1st Lt. W. C. Mulkey	352 FG	487 FS	Crashed during form-up, Bodney	Killed
P-51C-1-NT	42-103007	2nd Lt. C. R. Moritz	496 FG	555 FS	Midair with 42-103036	Killed
P-51C-1-NT	42-103036	2nd Lt. R. H. Magnuson	496 FG	555 FS	Midair with 42-103007	Returned to service
Write-offs						
3 unidentified P-47Ds—56 FG, 62 FS; 1 unidentified P-51—355 FG, 357 FS						
A-20B-DL	41-3370					
P-47D-5-RE	42-8508					
P-47D-15-RE	42-76189					
P-47C-5-RE	41-6533					
P-47D-2-RA	42-2282					
P-51B-15-NA	42-106903					
L-4B-PI	43-0698					
June 8						
B-24J-105-CO	42-109830	1st Lt. J. Q. Ogden	446 BG	704 BS	Bailed out near Isle of Chausey	5 KIA, 5 POW
B-17G-1-BO	42-31114	1st Lt. E. G. Sechrist	390 BG	568 BS	Margny-aux-Cérises, France	1 KIA, 1 POW, 8 evaded
B-24H-20-FO	42-94927	2nd Lt. T. I. Digges	493 BG	860 BS	Éréac, France	1 KIA, 2 POW, 7 evaded
P-47D-5-RE	42-8427	1st Lt. R. W. Engle	356 FG	361 FS	Le Tréport, France	Killed
P-47D-22-RE	42-26253	2nd Lt. R. A. Coughenour	356 FG	359 FS	Ditched, North Sea	Killed
P-47D-11-RE	42-75556	F/O E. L. Decker	356 FG	361 FS	25 miles south of Beauvais	Killed

Model	Serial	Name	Squadron	Group	Location	Fate
P-47D-15-RE	42-76168	1st Lt. J. B. Smith	359 FS	356 FG	Morlancourt, France	Evaded
P-47D-20-RE	42-76422	1st Lt. E. P. Lee Jr.	361 FS	356 FG	Omiécourt, France	Killed
P-47D-20-RE	42-76431	2nd Lt. J. Obosla	360 FS	356 FG	Lavilletertre, France	Killed
P-51B-15-NA	42-106823	2nd Lt. E. G. Allen	334 FS	4 FG	Midair 43-7150 near Le Mans, France	Evaded
P-51B-10-NA	43-7150	2nd Lt. J. F. Scott	334 FS	4 FG	Midair 42-106823 near Le Mans, France	Killed
P-51C-1-NT	42-103299	1st Lt. R. C. Smith	503 FS	339 FG	La Réhorie, France	Killed
P-51B-10-NA	42-106353	2nd Lt. J. F. Sawicki Jr.	505 FS	339 FG	La Touche, France	Killed
P-51B-10-NA	42-106699	1st Lt. P. H. Ewing	505 FS	339 FG	Le Cruchet, France	Evaded
P-51C-5-NT	42-103336	1st Lt. T. P. Fahrenwald	486 FS	352 FG	Louviers, France	Evaded
P-51B-5-NA	43-6988	1st Lt. H. L. Miller Jr.	328 FS	352 FG	Les Cambres at Fresquiennes, France	Killed
P-51B-15-NA	43-24801	2nd Lt. J. Campbell	328 FS	352 FG	Thionville-sur-Opton, France	Killed
P-51B-5-NA	43-6879	1st Lt. D. A. Donovan	358 FS	355 FG	Montboyer, France	Evaded
P-51B-10-NA	43-7164	Lt. Col. G. J. Dix	358 FS	355 FG	Les Artigues-de-Lussac, France	POW
P-51B-5-NA	43-6379	1st Lt. O. E. Harris Jr.	362 FS	357 FG	English Channel, rescued	Returned to service
P-51B-10-NA	42-106679	1st Lt. J. H. Oliphint	369 FS	359 FG	La Flèche, near Le Mans, France	Evaded
P-51B-15-NA	42-106898	1st Lt. B. M. Hagan III	368 FS	359 FG	Verneuil-sur-Avre, France	POW
P-51B-15-NA	42-106906	2nd Lt. R. B. Sander	369 FS	359 FG	Sainte-Anne, France	Killed
P-51B-10-NA	43-7199	1st Lt. R. J. Booth	369 FS	359 FG	La Flèche, near Le Mans, France	POW
P-51B-5-NA	43-6982	Capt. J. D. Hastin	374 FS	361 FG	Anet, France	POW
F-5A-10-LO	42-12981	Capt. R. P. Nelson	14 PRS	7 PRG	Flak, Eindhoven-Gestel, the Netherlands	Killed
F-5B-1-LO	42-67366	Capt. C. G. Cassaday	27 PRS	7 PRG	Flak, Eindhoven-Gestel, the Netherlands	Killed
Other Losses						
B-17G-30-DL	42-38185	2nd Lt. Fred Taylor	526 BS	379 BG	Landing gear collapse, Kimbolton	9 Returned to service
B-24J-125-CO	42-110026	Capt. J. P. Sullivan	713 BS	448 BG	One-wheel landing, RAF Woodbridge	10 Returned to service
B-24H-15-CF	41-29445	Lt. W. Sell	791 BS	467 BG	Hard landing, Attlebridge	10 Returned to service
B-24J-140-CO	42-110169	1st Lt. F. E. Sharp	854 BS	491 BG	Crashed on field attempting go-around, Metfield	9 Killed
B-24J-150-CO	44-40237		854 BS	491 BG	Destroyed on ground at Metfield by 42-110169	None
B-24J-150-CO	44-40240		854 BS	491 BG	Destroyed on ground at Metfield by 42-110169	None
B-17G-40-BO	42-97132	2nd Lt. C. H. Bryant	562 BS	388 BG	Impacted terrain 1 mile short of Knettishall	10 Killed

Eighth Air Force

Type	Serial	Pilot	Group	Squadron	Target/Area	Crew Status
June 8						
B-24H-10-FO	42-52117	2nd Lt. W. F. Moseley	486 BG	833 BS	Engines out, crashed Beckwithers Farm, Gosfield	8 Killed, 2 returned to service
B-24H-20-CF	42-50294	1st Lt. R. H. Heath	490 BG	849 BS	Collided with 42-94862 on landing at RAF Feltwell	10 Returned to service
B-24H-20-FO	42-94894	1st Lt. W. F. Brown	490 BG	849 BS	Unable to see taxiway at RAF Feltwell, rear-ended by 42-50294	9 Returned to service
B-24H-20-FO	42-94862	1st Lt. F. Borman	490 BG	849 BS	Instructed to land on closed runway, RAF Boscombe Down	10 Returned to service
P-51B-5-NA	43-6433	2nd Lt. J. T. Byrd Jr.	4 FG	334 FS	Controlled flight into terrain, Little Glenham, Suffolk	Killed
P-51B-10-NA	43-7149	F/O E. R. Williams	355 FG	358 FS	Flak, Bordeaux, France; crashed Eyeworth, Bedfordshire	Killed
Write-offs						
P-47C-2-RE	41-6266					
P-47D-22-RE	42-26295					
P-47D-21-RA	43-25555					
P-47D-1-RE	42-7913					
P-51B-15-NA	42-106947					
P-51B-15-NA	42-106806					
P-51C-5-NT	42-103359					
F-5B-1-LO	42-67382					

Ninth Air Force

Type	Serial	Pilot	Group	Squadron	Target/Area	Crew Status
June 6						
A-20G-35-DO	43-9904	1st Lt. R. L. Goodchild	410 BG	646 BS	Flak, Longpré-les-Corps-Saints, France	1 KIA, 2 POW
A-20G-35-DO	43-10148	2nd Lt. C. Church	416 BG	669 BS	Flak, marshalling yards, Forges, France	3 POW
A-20G-35-DO	43-10164	2nd Lt. R. A. Wipperman	416 BG	671 BS	Flak, marshalling yards, Forges, France	2 KIA, 1 POW
A-20J-10-DO	43-10128	1st Lt. R. T. Winn	409 BG	642 BS	Flak, Valognes, France	2 KIA, 2 POW
A-20J-15-DO	43-21468	Maj. M. W. Campbell	416 BG	669 BS	Flak, marshalling yards, Forges, France	3 POW, 1 evaded
B-26B-30-MA	41-31961	Maj. P. J. Stach	323 BG	455 BS	Flak, Caen, France	4 KIA, 3 POW
B-26B-50-MA	42-95902	2nd Lt. J. B. McKamey	344 BG	497 BS	Flak, Cherbourg Peninsula	6 KIA
F-6C-NA	43-12156	1st Lt. C. E. Stone	67 TRG	109 TRS	Flak at Vire, Normandy, France	Killed
F-6C-NA	43-12338	2nd Lt. R. L. Curtis	67 TRG	109 TRS	Kervénarc'hant, France	Killed
P-38J-10-LO	42-67511	2nd Lt. R. J. Belford	474 FG	430 FS	Ground fire, Périers, France	Killed
P-38J-15-LO	42-104133	Maj. L. B. Temple Jr.	474 FG	430 FS	Ground fire, Saint-Georges-de-Bohon, France	Killed
P-47D-10-RE	42-75168	2nd Lt. J. J. Martell	365 FG	338 FS	Own bomb blast, Courpeville, France	Killed
P-47D-15-RE	42-76203	1st Lt. R. L. Shipe	365 FG	385 FS	Own bomb blast, Saint-Sauveur de-Pierrepont, France	Killed
P-47D-20-RA	43-25278	2nd Lt. J. R. LaRochelle	371 FG	404 FS	Granville, France	POW
P-47D-20-RE	42-76368	2nd Lt. W. J. McGowan	366 FG	391 FS	Flak from train, St. Lô, France	Killed
P-47D-22-RE	42-26292	1st Lt. A. T. Krause	366 FG	390 FS	Flak, Bayeux, France	Killed
Airborne Assault Aircraft						
C-47	Unknown	Capt. E. B. Ours Jr.	435 TCG	78 TCS	Operation Elmira, flak, ditched English Channel	4 Returned to service
C-47	Unknown	Lt. S. Rutberg	435 TCG	78 TCS	Operation Elmira, flak, ditched English Channel	4 Returned to service
C-47-DL	41-38698	1st Lt. W. S. Butler	313 TCG	29 TCS	Flak, Carentan area	2 POW, 2 evaded
C-47A	Unknown	Maj. K. L. Glassburn	442 TCG	304 TCS	Flak; ditched into Bay of the Seine, France	5 Returned to service
C-47A-1-DK	42-92415	2nd Lt. J. J. Prince	442 TCG	303 TCS	Flak; crashed near Valognes, France	1 POW, 3 evaded
C-47A-5-DK	42-92462	1st Lt. S. B. Williams Jr.	442 TCG	304 TCS	Crashed near Sainte-Mère-Église, France	5 KIA
C-47A-15-DK	42-92868	1st Lt. W. R. Roycraft	313 TCG	49 TCS	Surtainville, France	5 KIA, 1 MIA
C-47A-15-DK	42-92894	Lt. Cromie	438 TCG		Flak; crashed in landing zone	4 Returned to service
C-47A-15-DK	42-92845	Unknown	441 TCC		Missing	5 MIA

Ninth Air Force

Type	Serial	Pilot	Group	Squadron	Target/Area	Crew Status
June 6						
C-47A-20-DK	42-93002	Capt. C. S. Cartwright	314 TCG	62 TCS	Flak, Étienville, France	5 Returned to service
C-47A-20-DK	42-93095	1st Lt. H. A. Capelluto	439 TCG	91 TCS	Flak; exploded in midair, Barneville, France	22 KIA
C-47A-30-DL	42-23638	1st Lt. W. R. Hitztaler	61 TCG	14 TCS	Flak near Valognes, France	2 KIA
C-47A-40-DL	42-24077	1st Lt. J. J. Hamblin	435 TCG	77 TCS	Flak southwest of Sainte-Mère-Église; 17 paratroopers	21 KIA
C-47A-60-DL	43-30734	Capt. J. H. Schaefers	435 TCG	77 TCS	Flak, Picauville, France; 5 crew, 17 paratroopers	19 KIA, 3 returned to service
C-47A-60-DL	43-30735	Capt. S. M. Malakoff	435 TCG	75 TCS	Flak, Sainte-Mère-Église; 18 paratroops deployed	5 KIA
C-47A-70-DL	42-100803	1st Lt. J. A. Lawson	437 TCG	84 TCS	Spatial disorientation in clouds, Normandy, France	4 KIA
C-47A-70-DL	42-100819	1st Lt. M. F. Sargent	439 TCG	91 TCS	Flak; crashed at Picauville, France	20 KIA
C-47A-70-DL	42-100733	1st Lt. W. H. Zeuner	440 TCG	96 TCS	Crashed into sea, Pointe de la Percée, France	18 KIA, 4 returned to service
C-47A-70-DL	42-100735	2nd Lt. W. J. McGillis	440 TCG	97 TCS	Flak; crashed into Bay of the Seine	4 Returned to service
C-47A-70-DL	42-100876	2nd Lt. M. F. Muir	439 TCG	93 TCS	Flak; crashed Beuzeville-la-Bastille, France	6 KIA, 17 paratroops returned
C-47A-75-DL	42-100905	1st Lt. R. B. Pullen	440 TCG	97 TCS	Flak; crashed at Le Fétage at Magneville, France	22 KIA
C-47A-75-DL	42-100914	2nd Lt. A. R. Keller	440 TCG	96 TCS	Flak; crashed into the sea of invasion beaches	4 KIA
C-47A-75-DL	42-101006	1st Lt. Doering	441 TCG	99 TCS	Controlled flight into terrain, Sainte-Mère-Église, France	4 Returned to service
C-47A-75-DL	42-101019	Capt. J. D. McCue	441 TCG	100 TCS	Flak; crashed Point-du Hoc, France	22 KIA
C-47A-75-DL	42-101025	2nd Lt. E. F. Hennig	441 TCG	301 TCS	Crashed Varenguebec, France	22 KIA
C-47A-80-DL	43-15101	2nd Lt. R. C. Howard	434 TCG	71 TCS	Ground fire, Étienville, France; was towing glider	5 Returned to service
C-53D-DO	42-68694	1st Lt. M. L. Burelbach	313 TCG	49 TCS	Flak; ditched in English Channel	4 Returned to service
C-53D-DO	42-68734	1st Lt. G. A. Briner	435 TCG	75 TCS	Operation Elmira; flak; ditched in English Channel	4 Returned to service
CG-4-GE	43-41047	F/O R. J. Powers	437 TCG	86 TCS	Tow rope broke; crashed Les Pieux, France	2 KIA, 2 returned to service
CG-4A	Unknown	Lt. Col. M. Murphy	434 TCG		Hiesville Drop Zone, landed hot	4 KIA, 2 MIA
CG-4A	Unknown	1st Lt. W. D. Laird	434 TCG		Les Pieux, Le Vrétot, near Cherbourg, France	4 POW
CG-4A	Unknown	F/O J. Larkin	437 TCG		Crashed Quettetot, France	5 Evaded
CG-4A	Unknown	F/O J. M. Lauri	437 TCG		Crashed Saint-Germain-le-Gaillard, France	5 Evaded
CG-4A	Unknown	F/O J. H. Mills	438 TCG	89 TCS	Near Blosville, France	4 KIA
CG-4A-FO	43-39990	F/O L. T. Stull	434 TCG	74 TCS	Landed Houtteville, France	2 KIA, 2 returned to service

Type	Serial	Pilot	Group	Squadron	Remarks	Casualties
CG-4A-FO	43-40112	1st Lt. R. V. Bolan	437 TCG	86 TCS	Crashed at Saint-Germain-le Gaillard, France	1 KIA, 3 POW
CG-4A-FO	43-40196	F/O C. S. Carson Jr.	437 TCG		Crashed at Saint-Germain-le Gaillard, France	1 KIA, 2 evaded
CG-4A-FO	43-40197	F/O A. R. Loving	437 TCG	86 TCS	Turbulence; crashed at Le Vrétot, France	5 KIA
CG-4A-FO	43-40199	1st Lt. H. C. Brewster	437 TCG	84 TCS	Crashed at Le Vrétot, France	3 KIA, 1 evaded
CG-4A-PR	42-56506	F/O M. M. Bogue	434 TCG	73 TCS	Fate unknown	4 MIA
CG-4A-PR	43-41826	F/O I. J. Morales	434 TCG	74 TCS	Montmartin-en-Graignes, France	2 KIA, 2 returned to service
CG-4A-WO	42-79200	2nd Lt. S. M. Appleman	437 TCG	85 TCS	Landed safely, Sainte-Mère-Église, France	1 POW, 4 returned to service
HORSA	HG915	F/O R. M. Ketcham	434 TCG	72 TCS	Hiesville Drop Zone, Cherbourg Peninsula, France	8 POW
HORSA	Unknown	1st Lt. J. W. Herriage	435 TCG	77 TCS	Flak; Normandy beachhead area	2 KIA
HORSA	LJ161	F/O D. Salemme	437 TCG	83 TCS	Near Blosville, France	4 KIA, 1 returned to service
HORSA	LJ216	Unknown	437 TCG	83 TCS	Near Blosville, France	1 KIA
Accidents						
B-26B-55-MA	42-96050	1st Lt. W. T. Berger	394 BG	587 BS	Midair with B-26 42-96263, over Gillingham, Kent	6 Killed
B-26F-1-MA	42-96263	2nd Lt. C. W. Kline Jr.	394 BG	587 BS	Midair with 42-96050, over Gillingham, Kent	6 Killed
B-26F-1-MA	42-96249	2nd Lt. T. F. Jenkins	394 BG	584 BS	Midair with B-26 42-107592; crashed East Sussex	7 Killed
B-26C-45-MO	42-107592	1st Lt. T. J. Potts	394 BG	584 BS	Midair with 42-96249, crashed Battle, Sussex	5 Killed, 1 returned to service
P-38J-15-LO	43-28674	Capt. G. W. Reas	474 FG	430 FS	Flak damage, landed gear-up	1 Returned to service
P-47D-16-RE	42-76113	Lt. P. K. Eaton	36 FG	53 FS	Landed long, Kingsnorth	1 Returned to service
P-47D-20-RA	43-25308	2nd Lt. G. W. Fosdick	50 FG	10 FS	Ground fire before takeoff on a mission	1 Returned to service
P-47D-10-RE	42-75197	Unknown	365 FG	386 FS	Bomb hung up, shook loose on landing and exploded	1 Returned to service
P-47D-20-RE	42-76491	2nd Lt. C. E. King	404 FG	511 FS	Stalled on approach to RAF Christchurch, England	1 Killed
P-51B-15-NA	42-106939	1Lt J. Rody	354 FG	353 FS	Landed short, RAF Stoney Cross, England	1 Returned to service
C-47A-45-DL	42-24122	1st Lt. E. W. Knight	435 TCG	76 TCS	Runway collision with 42-100633, RAF Welford, England	4 Returned to service
C-47A-65-DL	42-100633	1st Lt. J. C. Shive	437 TCG	85 TCS	Runway collision with 42-24122, RAF Welford, England	4 Returned to service
June 7						
B-26B-50-MA	42-95848	2nd Lt. L. R. Sullivan	391 BG	575 BS	Railroad target; flak; crashed Flers, France	4 KIA, 2 returned to service
A-20J-35-DL	43-10205	2nd Lt. J. J. Metz	410 BG	645 BS	Flak ignited left engine; blew up over English Channel	3 KIA
A-20J-15-DO	43-21715	Unknown	410 BG		MIA	MIA

Ninth Air Force

Type	Serial	Pilot	Group	Squadron	Target/Area	Crew Status
June 7						
P-47D-20-RE	42-25708	2nd Lt. S. E. Ragland Jr.	50 FG	313 FS	Shot down, possibly by Bf 109s, into English Channel	1 KIA
P-47D-20-RE	42-76537	1st Lt. N. T. Johnson	48 FG	492 FS	Small arms fire; belly-landed Turqueville, France	1 Returned to service
P-47D	Unknown	2nd Lt. R. M. Woodside	50 FG	10 FS	Ditched, Bay of the Seine, France	1 Returned to service
P-47D-21-RE	42-25339	Capt. C. F. Gee III	362 FG	379 FS	Shot down by Fw 190s, Fierville-les-Parcs, France	Killed
P-47D-11-RE	42-75267	2nd Lt. C. A. Gilbert	362 FG	378 FS	Shot down by Bf 109s, Écouché, France	Killed
P-47D-20-RE	42-76573	1st Lt. T. D. Jensen	362 FG	379 FS	Shot down by Fw 190s, Lisieux, France	Killed
P-47D	Unknown	Lt. R. D. Day	362 FG	377 FS	Ground fire; bailed out over English Channel	1 Returned to service
P-47D-2-RA	42-22749	2nd Lt. C. S. Voigt	365 FG	377 FS	Belly landing, Montsurvent, France	1 Evaded
P-47D-22-RE	42-26128	1st Lt. H. M. Jones	365 FG	386 FS	Flak; bailed out Saint-Sauveur-Lendelin, France	1 KIA
P-47D-10-RE	42-75044	1st Lt. E. J. McKnight	365 FG	388 FS	Own bomb blast; crashed Saint-Martin-des-Besaces, France	1 KIA
P-47D-15-RE	42-76252	2nd Lt. G. T. Wark	365 FG	386 FS	Hit tree while strafing; Isigny-sur-Mer, France	1 POW
P-47D-15-RE	42-76355	1st Lt. M. T. Stelle	365 FG	387 FS	Controlled flight into terrain, Le Tourneur, France	1 KIA
P-47D-20-RE	42-76472	2nd Lt. C. G. Arledge	365 FG	386 FS	Ground fire; crashed Saint-Sauveur-Lendelin, France	1 KIA
P-47D-22-RE	42-26017	2nd Lt. A. M. Wood	366 FG	389 FS	Armored recon mission; bailed out	1 KIA
P-47D-11-RE	42-75431	Unknown	366 FG		MIA	1 MIA
P-47D-15-RE	42-76260	2nd Lt. H. H. Hornbeck	366 FG	391 FS	Own bomb blast; crashed Saint-Clair-sur-l'Elle, France	1 KIA
P-47D-15-RE	42-76309	2nd Lt. Henry G. Hyde	366 FG	390 FS	Hit by ground fire, strafing in the Balleroy area, France	1 KIA
P-47D-20-RE	42-76375	2nd Lt. Paul W. Luthy	366 FG	390 FS	Struck by own bomb blast, Grandcamp area, France	1 POW
P-47D-20-RE	42-76574	2nd Lt. John L. Hustis	366 FG	389 FS	Crashed near La Courbe, France	1 KIA
P-47D-22-RE	42-26262	2nd Lt. Norman E. Langmaid	369 FG	397 FS	Ground fire while strafing; crashed Mestry, France	1 KIA
P-47D-15-RE	42-75819	2nd Lt. Joe C. Howard	368 FG	397 FS	Ground fire while strafing, crashed Le Molay, France	1 KIA
P-47D-15-RE	42-76194	2nd Lt. Buel W. Bates	368 FG	397 FS	Missing near Bayeaux, France	1 KIA
P-47D	Unknown	2Lt Richard O. Kirwin	373 FG	412 FS	Damaged by Me 109; bailed out, wounded	1 Returned to service
P-47D-2-RE	42-8379	1st Lt. Joseph H. Vivian	404 FG	506 FS	Lost near Grandcamp, France	1 KIA

Aircraft	Serial	Crew	Group	Squadron	Circumstances	Fate
P-47D-11-RE	42-75391	Capt. John E. Wilkes	406 FG	514 FS	Flak; crashed near Villers-Bocage, France	1 KIA
P-51B-5-NA	43-6517	2nd Lt. Leon A. C. Huffman	354 FG	353 FS	Failed to pull out of dive while bombing, Carentan, France	1 KIA
F-6C-NT	42-103230	Capt. Mauritz F. Johnson	67 TRG	15 TRS	Flak; crashed near Citerne, France	1 KIA
C-47A-80-DL	43-15335	Unknown	53 TCG	Unknown	Flak; ditched in English Channel, off Pointe de Barfleur	Unknown
C-47A-80-DL	43-15340	1st Lt. Richard B. Frost	61 TCG	14 TCS	Flak; ditched in English Channel	1 KIA, 3 returned to service
C-47A-15-DK	42-92897	Unknown	61 TCG	Unknown	Flak; ditched in English Channel	4 Returned to service
C-47-DL	42-5699	1st Lt. Kermit R. Robinson	313 TCG	49 TCS	Flak; ditched in English Channel	5 Returned to service
C-47A-80-DL	43-15165	1st Lt. Samuel M. Willis Jr.	313 TCG	49 TCS	Flak; ditched in English Channel	4 Returned to service
C-47A-85-DL	43-15101	Maj. Edgar F. Stovall	313 TCG	48 TCS	Flak; crashed at Amfreville, France	6 POW, 1 evaded
C-47A-90-DL	43-15637	Capt. Claude J. Wilson	313 TCG	49 TCS	Crashed in swamp, Cherbourg Peninsula, France	3 KIA, 2 POW, 2 evaded
C-47-DL	41-38679	2nd Lt. George Risley Jr.	314 TCG	32 TCS	Midair with C-47 43-15146, Sébeville, France	4 KIA
C-47A-20-DK	42-93065	Capt. Howard W. Sass	314 TCG	50 TCS	Flak; crashed near Sainte-Mère-Église	4 KIA, 1 returned to service
C-47A-80-DL	43-15146	Capt. Robert Bennett	314 TCG	32 TCS	Midair with C-47 41-38679, Sébeville, France	5 POW
C-47A-80-DL	43-15169	Unknown	435 TCG	Unknown	Flak; ditched in English Channel	Unknown
C-47A-45-DL	42-24099	Lt. Seymour Rutberg	435 TCG		Satan's Sanctuary II; flak; ditched in English Channel	4 returned via HMS Skate
CG-4A-PR	42-256539	F/O Dale R. Cole	435 TCG	77 TCS	Crashed south of Sainte-Mère-Église, France	1 KIA
C-47A-10-DK	42-108870	Unknown	437 TCG	Unknown	Damaged by flak during Mission Elmira	5 Returned to service
Horsa	LG998	F/O Marvin A. Lauen	437 TCG	86 TCS	Crashed near Hiesville, France	1 KIA
C-47A-80-DL	43-15078	1st Lt. Jerome M. McQuaid	440 TCG	97 TCS	Flak; ditched in English Channel	4 Returned to service
C-47A-75-DL	42-100902	2nd Lt. John P. Goodwin	440 TCG	95 TCS	Struck by Allied bombs in flight; ditched in English Channel	4 KIA, 4 returned to service
C-47A-80-DL	43-15119	Unknown	442 TCG	Unknown	Flak; ditched in English Channel off Saint-Marcouf	Unknown
Horsa	HS129	F/O Steve P. Odahowski	434 TCG	71 TCS	Landed near Hiesville; 2 killed by ground fire	4 KIA, 5 POW
Horsa	LG834	2nd Lt. Ernest D. McMillen Jr.	435 TCG	75 TCS	Crash-landed; hit Rommel Asparagus, Sainte-Mère-Église	2 KIA, 2 POW, 8 returned to service
CG-4A-GE	43-40145	1st Lt. Raymond E. Darling Jr.	438 TCG	83 TCS	Landed near Sainte-Mère-Église; pinned down	2 KIA, 1 returned to service
C-47A-70-DL	42-100735	2nd Lt. William J. McGillis	440 TCG	97 TCS	Flak; ditched in English Channel; picked up by PT boat	4 Returned to service
CG-4A-GE	43-19874	F/O Hubert W. Lindsey	441 TCG	100 TCS	Crashed near Sainte-Mère-Église, France	1 KIA, 1 returned to service

RAF Bomber Command

Type	Serial	Pilot	Squadron	Target/Area	Crew Status
June 5/6					
Halifax III	LW382	F/O J. F. T. Beesley, RCAF	426 Sqn	Houlgate	7 KIA
Halifax III	NA511	P/O C. S. Baldwin	77 Sqn	Maisy	7 Injured
Halifax III	LW638	P/O S. A. D. Walker	76 Sqn	Mont Fleury	7 KIA
Halifax III	MZ513	S/L W. G. Watson	578 Sqn	Mont Fleury	4 KIA, 3 survivors
Lancaster I	LL833	P/O M. J. Steele, RNZAF	101 Sqn	D-Day support	8 Survivors
Lancaster III	NE166	S/L A. W. Raybould	582 Sqn	Longues	7 KIA
Lancaster III	ND874	P/O R. G. Ward, RAAF	50 Sqn	St. Pierre	6 KIA, 1 evaded
Lancaster III	ND739	W/C E. J. Carter	97 Sqn	St. Pierre	7 KIA
Lancaster III	ND815	Lt. F. V. Jespersen, RNAF	97 Sqn	St. Pierre	7 KIA
Mosquito VI	NS950	S/L Shaw	515 Sqn	Bomber support	2 KIA
Mosquito VI	PZ189	S/L W. R. Butterfield	515 Sqn	Bomber support	2 KIA
Stirling III	LJ621	P/O W. H. Mayo	149 Sqn	D-Day support	6 KIA, 2 POW, 1 evaded
Stirling III	LK385	S/L C. J. K. Hutchins	149 Sqn	D-Day support	9 KIA
June 6/7					
Halifax III	MZ619	Sgt. A. A. Waller	578 Sqn	Châteaudun	7 KIA
Halifax III	LW377	F/S C. A. Selfe, RCAF	426 Sqn	Coutances	7 Survivors
Lancaster I	ME556	P/O T. M. J. Shervington	550 Sqn	Achéres	7 KIA
Lancaster I	ME579	F/S C. R. King	9 Sqn	Argentan	6 KIA, 1 survivor
Lancaster I	LL783	F/L K. Roberts, RAAF	619 Sqn	Caen	5 KIA, 2 POW
Lancaster I	ME811	F/O G. E. J. Bain, RCAF	576 Sqn	Vire	1 KIA, 1 POW, 5 evaded
Lancaster II	DS768	F/O D. T. Ryan	408 Sqn	Coutances	7 Survivors
Lancaster III	ND519	F/L W. A. Stratis	44 Sqn	Caen	7 KIA
Lancaster III	ND467	F/O G. M. Kennedy, RNZAF	83 Sqn	Caen	6 KIA, 1 evaded
Lancaster III	ND685	P/O A. W. Wilson, RAAF	630 Sqn	Caen	4 KIA, 3 POW
Lancaster III	ND680	S/L E. Sprawson	106 Sqn	Coutances	2 KIA, 2 POW, 3 evaded
Lancaster III	NE150	P/O M. G. M. Warren	106 Sqn	Coutances	5 KIA, 1 evaded, 1 survivor

Aircraft	Serial	Crew	Squadron	Target	Casualties
Lancaster III	LM533	F/O J. W. Wesley	115 Sqn	Lisieux	7 KIA
Lancaster III	NE173	F/L W. H. Way, RCAF	103 Sqn	Vire	7 KIA
Lancaster III	JB700	P/O F. J. Knight, RAAF	460 Sqn	Vire	7 KIA
June 7/8					
Halifax III	NA505	F/O H. R. Jones, RCAF	420 Sqn	Achéres	8 KIA
Halifax III	LV987	WO2 D. F. Foster, RCAF	427 Sqn	Achéres	2 POW, 6 evaded
Halifax III	LW128	S/L W. D. Anderson, RCAF	429 Sqn	Achéres	1 KIA, 2 POW, 1 evaded, 3 survivors
Halifax III	LW582	F/O W. K. Vickerman, RCAF	422 Sqn	Achéres	1 KIA, 2 POW, 4 evaded
Halifax III	MZ531	Sgt. P. R. Hunt, RCAF	76 Sqn	Juvisy	5 POW, 2 evaded
Halifax III	LV868	F/L D. Davies	76 Sqn	Juvisy	1 KIA, 6 survivors
Halifax III	MZ568	F/O J. A. Cole, RCAF	78 Sqn	Juvisy	7 KIA
Halifax III	MZ577	F/S M. McLear, RCAF	78 Sqn	Juvisy	2 KIA, 5 POW
Halifax III	MZ636	F/L G. A. Marrows	78 Sqn	Juvisy	7 KIA
Halifax III	MZ283	F/S W. R. Pearce	466 Sqn	Juvisy	7 KIA
Halifax III	LK760	F/S T. H. Sinclair, RNZAF	158 Sqn	Versailles	7 Survivors
Halifax III	LK863	P/O I. V. Seddon, RAAF	158 Sqn	Versailles	7 Evaded
Halifax III	MZ602	P/O J. P. Artyniuk, RCAF	431 Sqn	Versailles	8 KIA
Halifax III	LK866	P/O I. M. Hamilton, RCAF	640 Sqn	Versailles	2 KIA, 4 POW, 1 evaded
Halifax V	LL306	F/L H. C. Jones, RAAF	138 Sqn	SIS	7 KIA
Halifax V	LL390	S/L M. A. Brogan	138 Sqn	SOE	7 Survivors
Halifax V	LL416	P/O F. H. Lyne, RCAF	138 Sqn	SOE	6 KIA, 1 evaded
Halifax V	LL466	F/S A. D. MacKay, RCAF	138 Sqn	SOE	7 KIA
Lancaster I	HK548	P/O E. A. Law, RAAF	115 Sqn	Chevreuse	2 KIA, 5 evaded
Lancaster I	HK552	F/S J. E. Todd, RAAF	115 Sqn	Chevreuse	6 KIA, 1 evaded
Lancaster I	LL864	P/O R. P. Maude	115 Sqn	Chevreuse	7 KIA
Lancaster I	ME565	P/O A. L. Arnell, RCAF	101 Sqn	Cerisy-la-Forêt	7 KIA
Lancaster I	LL781	F/L W. J. Bell	15 Sqn	Massy-Palaiseau	1 KIA, 6 survivors
Lancaster I	LL945	F/L W. E. Palmer	15 Sqn	Massy-Palaiseau	7 KIA

APPENDIX VI

Select D-Day Survivors

VESSELS

HMS *Belfast* (C35)

River Thames, London—public view

The keel for HMS *Belfast*, one of ten Town Class cruisers, was laid in December 1936. She was launched less than two years later, on March 17, 1938. On June 6, 1944, HMS *Belfast* began shelling the coast at 5:27 a.m., suppressing fire from German coastal guns at La Marefontaine at Ver-sur-Mer. She remained on station until June 16, providing fire support and tending to the wounded before a short replenishment. HMS *Belfast* continued to bombard targets on the mainland until June 23, when the battle had moved inland, out of the reach of her guns.

NARA 80-G-633833

HMCS *Haida* (G-63)

Hamilton, Ontario, Canada—public view; pc.gc.ca/en/lhn-nhs/on/haida

This Tribal Class destroyer of the Canadian Navy sailed as part of the 10th Destroyer Flotilla operating out of Plymouth, England, during spring 1944. Her duty was to destroy as many enemy vessels as possible to reduce the risk to the D-Day invasion fleet.

LCT-7074

Portsmouth, England—under restoration; nmrn.org.uk/LCT7074

LCT-7074 is the last of her type in the United Kingdom and a veteran of the D-Day campaign. More than 800 LCTs participated in the D-Day invasion, delivering 10 tanks for the British 7th Armoured Division ("the Desert Rats"). *LCT-7074* had gone derelict at Birkenhead, England, and sank at her moorings. In October 2014, she was raised and transported to the naval base at Portsmouth for conservation and eventual restoration.

LST-325

lstmemorial.org

Beginning with the D-Day assault through the end of the war, *LST-325* made forty-three round-trips between England and the Omaha, Utah, Gold, and Juno invasion beaches, as well as the port at Rouen, France. In December 1944, *LST-325* rescued more than 700 men from the torpedoed troop transport *Empire Javelin*.

LST-393

lst393.org

This LST arrived off Omaha Beach on June 7 and discharged US Army soldiers and vehicles. She then took on casualties and began her first round-trip on June 8. *LST-393* made thirty round-trips to the invasion beaches in Normandy during the invasion and subsequent race to Germany.

PHOTO BY ARTHUR CASADONTE

SS *Jeremiah O'Brien*

ssjeremiahobrien.org

The *Jeremiah O'Brien* is the last unaltered Liberty ship. She supported the D-Day invasion, making eleven round-trips between Normandy and England. The ship returned to Normandy on the fiftieth anniversary of the D-Day invasion in 1994.

PHOTO BY NICHOLAS A. VERONICO

USS *Laffey* (DD-724)

laffey.org

Destroyer *Laffey* arrived off Utah Beach at dawn on D-Day to screen the invasion ships and bombard coastal defense guns. One June 12, *Laffey* engaged with German E-boats.

USS *Texas* (BB-35)

battleshiptexas.org
tpwd.texas.gov/state-parks/battleship
-texas/park_history

The battleship *Texas* provided gunfire support to troops going ashore on D-Day. During the ensuing days, *Texas* was struck by two German coast artillery shells. The first killed one sailor and injured a dozen more; the second shell failed to explode.

NAVAL HISTORICAL CENTER NH 107015

AIRBORNE ASSAULT AIRCRAFT: C-47 SKYTRAINS

C-47A-1-DL 42-23310

Private owner • Flyable

Flew as a glider tug with the 75th Troop Carrier Squadron, 435th Troop Carrier Group on D-Day.

C-47A-1-DL 42-24064, *Placid Lassie*

Tunison Foundation Inc. • Flyable

This aircraft flew with the 74th Troop Carrier Squadron as part of the Chicago mission, towing CG-4A Waco gliders carrying members of the 101st Airborne Division.

PHOTO BY PARR YONEMOTO

C-47A-15-DK 42-92841, *Turf and Sport Special*

Air Mobility Command Museum, Dover, Delaware • Preserved, on public view

This Skytrain flew with the 61st Troop Carrier Squadron on D-Day, dropping paratroopers from the 82nd Airborne Division near Sainte-Mère-Église.

PHOTO BY IAN E. ABBOTT

C-47A-15-DK 42-92847, *That's All, Brother*

Commemorative Air Force • Flyable

C-47A 42-92847, *That's All, Brother* was the lead ship of the Normandy aerial invasion that saw more than 800 other Skytrains drop over 13,000 Allied paratroopers behind enemy lines. *That's All, Brother* went on to support Operations Market Garden (Eindhoven and Nijmegen, the Netherlands), Repulse (supplying troops at Bastogne), and Varsity (crossing the Rhine River) before being sold as surplus at the end of the war. This Skytrain was slated to be scrapped before being rescued by the Commemorative Air Force.

PHOTO BY PARR YONEMOTO

C-47A-20-DK 42-93096

National World War II Museum, New Orleans, Louisiana • Preserved, on public view

nationalww2museum.org

This aircraft dropped pathfinders of the 2nd Battalion, 508th Parachute Infantry Regiment, 82nd Airborne Division, on D-Day.

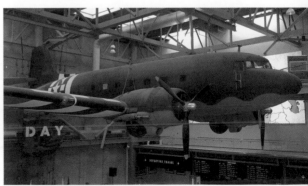

PHOTO BY NICHOLAS A. VERONICO

C-47A-65-DL 42-100521, *Night Fright*

Private owner • Under restoration

Night Fright flew with the 436th Troop Carrier Group.

C-47A-65-DL 42-100591, *Tico Belle*

Valiant Air Command, Titusville, Florida • Flyable

valiantaircommand.com

Dropped members of the 82nd Airborne Division near Sainte-Mère-Église on D-Day.

PHOTO BY PARR YONEMOTO

C-47A-70-DL 42-100825, *Argonia*

Airborne Museum, Sainte-Mère-Église, France • Preserved, on public view

C-47A-75-DL 42-100882, *Drag 'em Oot*

Private owner • Flyable

Flew two missions on D-Day, the first dropping paratroopers from the 82nd Airborne Division near Sainte-Mère-Église.

C-47A-75-DL 42-100971

Dutch Dakota Association/DDA Classic Airliners, the Netherlands

dutchdakota.nl

This aircraft flew with the 316th Troop Carrier Group's 44th Troop Carrier Squadron on D-Day, dropping paratroopers of the 515th Parachute Infantry Regiment near Sainte-Mère-Église.

C-47A-80-DL 43-15073, *The SNAFU Special*

Association Merville-Dakota, France • Preserved, on public view

the-snafu-special.com

On D-Day, *The SNAFU Special* dropped members of the 501st Parachute Infantry Regiment, 101st Airborne Division, south of Sainte-Mère-Église and then continued to support the troops throughout the battle.

C-47-DL 43-30652, *Whiskey 7*

National Warplane Museum, Geneseo, New York • Flyable

nationalwarplanemuseum.com

Flew with the 316th Troop Carrier Group, dropping the 82nd Airborne Division near Sainte-Mère-*Église* on D-Day.

PHOTO BY PARR YONEMOTO

DOUGLAS C-53 SKYTROOPER

C-53D-DO 42-68710

Private owner • Under restoration

Flew with the 62nd Troop Carrier Squadron on D-Day, dropping members of the 2nd Battalion, 508th PIR, 82nd Airborne Division, near Sainte-Mère-Église.

England. Pen and Sword Military. 2012.

Veronico, Nicholas A. *Bloody Skies: US Eighth Air Force Battle Damage in World War II.* Mechanicsburg, Pennsylvania. Stackpole Books. 2014.

_____. *Hidden Warships: Finding World War II's Abandoned, Sunk, and Preserved Warships.* St. Paul, Minnesota. Zenith Press. 2015.

_____. *Hidden Warbirds: The Epic Stories of Finding, Recovering, and Rebuilding WWII's Lost Aircraft.* St. Paul, Minnesota. Zenith Press. 2013.

_____. *Hidden Warbirds II: More Epic Stories of Finding, Recovering, and Rebuilding WWII's Lost Aircraft.* St. Paul, Minnesota. Zenith Press. 2014.

Veronico, Nicholas A., and Armand H. Veronico. *Battlestations: American Warships of World War II in Color.* Osceola, Wisconsin. Motorbooks International. 2001.

Zaloga, Steven J. *D-Day 1944 (1) Omaha Beach.* Botley, Oxford, Great Britain. Osprey Publishing Ltd. 2003.

REPORTS

Peters, Brett (Major, USAR). *Mulberry-American: The Artificial Harbor at Omaha.* US Army Command and General Staff College. Fort Leavenworth, Kansas. 2011.

US Army. *Report on Beach Intelligence, "Operation Overlord," Normandy, France, North Coast, June 1944.* Intelligence Division, Office of the Chief Engineer, ETO, US Army.

ON THE INTERNET

D-Day–Related Sites

amphibiousforces.org
6juin1944.com
www.dday.center
dday-overlord.com
d-dayrevisited.co.uk
First Division Museum; fdmuseum.org
history.army.mil

ACKNOWLEDGMENTS

The 300 photos of the D-Day invasion between these covers are presented to memorialize the stories and sacrifices of those who fought for freedom seventy-five years in the past. Each image captures a moment in time for a soldier, sailor, or airman. Let us never forget the sacrifices they made.

I would like to thank the following for their assistance in preparing this volume: Ian Abbott, the Amphibious Forces Memorial Museum, Caroline and Ray Bingham, Clair and Joe Bradshaw, Roger Cain, Arthur Casadonte and Brett Casadonte, Gustavo Cornjo, Melissa and Darby Culler, Kev Darling, Ed Davies, Jim Dunn, Craig Fuller, Jerry Gilmartin, Wayne Gomes, Kevin Grantham, Ted Holgerson, Mark Hrutkay, William T. Larkins, Dale Messimer, Robert Nishimura, Stan Piet, Taigh Ramey, Debra Sanders, Lee Scales, Doug Scroggins, Justin Spielmann, Ron Strong, Scott Thompson, Rick Turner, Armand and Karen Veronico, Betty Veronico, Kathleen and Tony Veronico, Parr Yonemoto, Paulette Baker, and Emily Chiarelli. Special thanks to David Reisch and Stephanie Otto from Stackpole Books for the opportunity to present this work. Thank you all.

Any errors or omissions are completely my responsibility.

Nicholas A. Veronico
San Carlos, California

OTHER BOOKS BY NICHOLAS A. VERONICO

Pearl Harbor Air Raid: The Japanese Attack on the US Pacific Fleet, Dec. 7, 1941

Bloody Skies: US Eighth Air Force Battle Damage in World War II

Boneyard Nose Art

Military Aircraft Boneyards

AMARG: America's Military Aircraft Boneyard

Air Force One: The Aircraft of the Modern US Presidency

Spyplanes: The Illustrated Guide to Manned Reconnaissance and Surveillance Aircraft from World War I to Today

Hidden Warbirds: The Epic Stories of Finding, Recovering, and Restoring Lost Aircraft

Hidden Warbirds II: More Epic Stories of Finding, Recovering, and Restoring Lost Aircraft

Hidden Warships: Finding World War II's Abandoned, Sunk, and Preserved Warships

Battlestations! American Warships of World War II in Color

Images of America: World War II Shipyards by the Bay

Blue Angels: A Fly-by History: 60 Years of Aerial Excellence

Blue Angels: 50 Years of Precision Flight

21st Century US Airpower

1001 Aviation Facts

Giant Cargo Planes

Fly Past Fly Present: A Celebration of Preserved Aviation

Convair PB4Y-2/P4Y-2 Privateer

Vought F4U Corsair: The Combat, Development, and Racing History of the Corsair

Griffon-Powered Mustangs (Raceplanes Tech, Vol. 1)

Racing Bearcats and Corsairs (Raceplanes Tech, Vol. 2)

Wreckchasing: A Guide to Finding Aircraft Crash Sites

Wreckchasing 2: Commercial Aircraft Crashes

Wreckchasing 101: A Guide to Finding Aircraft Crashes and Crash Sites (with Ed Davies et al.)

Images of Aviation: Moffett Field

Travis Air Force Museum (A Guide to the Aircraft of)

March Field Museum (A Guide to the Aircraft of)

Castle Air Museum (A Guide to the Aircraft of)

Commercial Aviation

Airliners in Flight: A Gallery of Air-to-Air Photography

Boeing 377 Stratocruiser (Airliner Tech, Vol. 9)

Convair Twins (Airliner Tech, Vol. 12)

Douglas DC-3: Sixty Years and Counting

Junkyard Jets

Local History

Images of America: San Carlos

Images of America: Redwood City

Redwood City: Then and Now

Images of America: Menlo Park

Art History

Depression-Era Sculpture of the Bay Area

Depression-Era Murals of the Bay Area